Pastoral Care with
Handicapped Persons

Creative Pastoral Care and Counseling Series
Editor: Howard J. Clinebell, Jr.
Associate Editor: Howard W. Stone

Pastoral Care with Handicapped Persons

Lowell G. Colston

Fortress Press   Philadelphia

COPYRIGHT © 1978 BY FORTRESS PRESS

———

Library of Congress Cataloging in Publication Data
Colston, Lowell G.
    Pastoral care with handicapped persons.
    (Creative pastoral care and counseling series)
    Bibliography: p.
    1. Church work with the handicapped. I. Title.
BV4460.C64   253   77-15229
ISBN 0-8006-0560-8

———

6516C78   Printed in the United States of America   1–560

Contents

Series Foreword

Let me share with you some of the hopes that are in the minds of those of us who helped to develop this series—hopes that relate directly to you as the reader. It is our desire and expectation that these books will be of help to you in developing better working tools as a minister-counselor. We hope that they will do this by encouraging your own creativity in developing more effective methods and programs for helping people live life more fully. It is our intention in this series to affirm the many things you have going for you as a minister in helping troubled persons —the many assets and resources from your religious heritage, your role as the leader of a congregation, and your unique relationship to individuals and families throughout the life cycle. We hope to help you reaffirm *the power of the pastoral* by the use of fresh models and methods in your ministry.

The aim of the series is not to be comprehensive with respect to topics but rather to bring innovative approaches to some major types of counseling. Although the books are practice-oriented, they also provide a solid foundation of theological and psychological insights. They are written primarily for ministers (and those preparing for the ministry) but we hope that they will also prove useful to other counselors who are interested in the crucial role of spiritual and value issues in all helping relationships. In addition we hope that the series will be useful in seminary courses, clergy support groups, continuing education workshops, and lay befriender training.

This is a period of rich new developments in counseling and psychotherapy. The time is ripe for a flowering of creative methods and insights in pastoral care and counseling. Our expectation is that this series will stimulate grass-roots creativity as innovative methods and programs come alive for you. Some of the major thrusts that will be discussed in this series include a new awareness of the unique contributions of the theologically trained counselor, the liberating power of the human potentials orientation, an appreciation of the pastoral care function of the ministering congregation, the importance of humanizing systems and institutions as well as close relationships, the importance of pastoral *care* (and not just counseling), the many opportunities for caring ministries throughout the life cycle, the deep changes in male-female relationships, and the new psychotherapies such as Gestalt therapy, Transactional Analysis, educative counseling, and crisis methods. Our hope is that this series will enhance your resources for your ministry to persons by opening doorways to understanding of these creative thrusts in pastoral care and counseling.

In this volume Lowell Colston shares the rich insights acquired through his long experience of teaching and practicing pastoral counseling. As you will discover, there is special depth to his understanding of physical disabilities. There is a firsthand power and authenticity about what he writes on this topic. Perhaps it is that, like stained-glass windows, the experience of being handicapped can best be understood from the inside. Much of the book was written during those long hours the author must spend each week connected to the kidney machine in order to survive. When he writes of the importance of the will to live and the continuing struggle between accepting and rejecting one's situation, Lowell is sharing his own experiences. I rejoice that he chose in this book to share these and many other precious learnings from his own painful struggles.

The author's philosophy and theology of disabilities undergirds the practical approaches to caring he describes; this basic understanding is clear and confronting: persons with disabilities are still essentially *persons* with potentialities which can be developed! Creative coping with a handicap involves discovering and developing the positive potentialities inherent in the handicap! Building on this foundation, Lowell sets forth a model of mutual care in which handicapped persons can give as well as receive caring. The model of pastoring he describes is called "pastoral advocacy." This involves standing with handicapped persons in strength, eliciting thereby their strength and resources, and then engaging in mutual ministry with them.

Responding constructively to physical disabilities is made more difficult by the many ways in which our society treats "the handicapped" as partial persons. The challenge to the church is to avoid mirroring and enhancing society's rejection and instead to make our churches genuine communities of mutual care. In such communities acceptance of the full personhood of those with major limitations becomes an experiential reality for them. The author makes it confrontingly clear that this acceptance is communicated most convincingly by the way a congregation implements practical plans for responding to the needs of disabled persons and their families.

This book will challenge church leaders to develop more effective and innovative mutual support systems for and with handicapped persons in their congregation and community. It will be of great value to pastors and other professionals who desire to relate more constructively with persons who are handicapped. Equally important, the book will also speak powerfully and helpfully to those who *are* handicapped and to their families and friends.

Most people have or will have some physical limitation sooner or later. All of us can learn invaluable lessons from those with major limitations. We can learn how to use our limitations (those reminders of our finitude) as challenges and resources for living with more caring, aliveness, and intentionality. On a personal level, I found that Lowell's sharing of his experiences confronted me with the need to respond to my own frustrating though relatively minor disability more growthfully.

Lowell Colston spent fourteen years as a parish pastor. He has taught at Christian Theological Seminary in Indianapolis for twenty years. Among his numerous valuable contributions to the literature of pastoral care this book is one of the most meaningful and significant. As you read these pages I hope that you will encounter yourself and find some liberating insights that will enable you to use your own limitations more creatively.

HOWARD J. CLINEBELL, JR.

Preface

Astonishing as it may seem, more than 30 million persons in the United States are physically and developmentally disabled.* Many of these people go relatively unnoticed except for an occasional glance by some passerby who may be struggling inwardly to avoid either hurting them or becoming involved with them. Nonhandicapped people are often unsure about how to relate to disabled persons. Rather than go through the embarrassment of learning what to say or what to do or how to feel, they simply ignore the handicapped and, wittingly or unwittingly, discriminate against them. Disabled persons therefore comprise a significant minority which, like many another minority group in our society, feels alienated.

Most regrettably, human resources get wasted in many ways. Attitudes toward disabled persons can often be more crippling than the affliction itself. With opportunity and encouragement, however, every disabled person can be a full person despite the disablement. A few can even achieve greatness. Former President Franklin Delano Roosevelt was stricken with poliomyelitis and spent much of his remarkable political life in a wheel chair. Helen Keller overcame a mute existence by learning to speak; she eventually contributed her consummate skill and boundless energy to conquering the handicap of deafness. Less well known but equally courageous people in many walks of life have turned their handicaps into "music." (The appropriateness of this metaphor will become apparent in chapter 1.)

Because many disabled persons do not see themselves as "handicapped," they resent being tagged with that label. They especially do not like to be pitied or "rescued." However, most handicapped persons appreciate thoughtful and considerate, even confrontive efforts on the part of people who exhibit trust and faith in their capacity to overcome the limitations imposed by their handicap.

Pastors and counselors have a responsibility to see and understand the so-called handicap from the point of view of the disabled or afflicted person. This can hardly be done without studied effort and developed skill in the active and intense art of listening imaginatively to what that person is saying about what he or she is experiencing.

The suffering every handicapped person goes through can potentially strengthen that person's endurance, ingenuity, and coping capacity. In many ways it challenges the person to grow and develop. It can make contributions of inestimable value to the quality of life. People who have experienced such suffering need not be social discards; indeed, they can be of greater rather than lesser value to society.

I am not saying that people should be encouraged purposely to contrive their own suffering. But coping with illnesses, accidents, and other afflictions can often teach caution, patience, perceptiveness, and wisdom—virtues which may often be hard to come by apart from the trial of suffering.

Pastoral care and counseling with handicapped persons can and should be a mutual enterprise, involving a giving and receiving on both sides. The word *with* in the title of this book is deliberately chosen; it says precisely what I mean to convey. Ministers and lay people alike are engaging in pastoral care when they enter into the suffering of disabled persons and experience the contagious spirit of their drive toward wholeness. The pastoral counseling approach recommended here is referred to as "abiding advocacy." By that I mean a continuing, unfailing, persistent standing by, or moving with, or entering into the sufferings of handicapped persons. I would underscore, however, that the counseling relationship involves a mutual ministry. Pastors get as much as they give.

I am grateful to the many persons who have contributed to my understanding of living with a handicap, especially my own team of doctors, Charles Carter, LeRoy King, and Daniel Ahearn; an attorney who has been a great source of inspiration to me, Claude

Spilman; psychologists at the rehabilitation center of the Community Hospital in Indianapolis, Richard Bost and Edward DeVries; my fellow churchman, Maurice Ireland; my friends and fellow clergy people, Dr. and Mrs. Waldo Savage of First Congregational Church (United Church of Christ) in Indianapolis; and another friend and clergyman, Harold H. Wilke, whose many gracious contributions are noted throughout this book.

Special thanks is due to Mrs. Barbara Somerville who read, criticized, helped to revise, and typed the manuscript. And a final word of gratitude goes to my wife, Frances, for monitoring my dialysis machine and for the many other ways she has supported this enterprise.

1. The Chastening Calamity of the "Cracked Case"

Recently I heard the story of how the lute, an ancient stringed instrument related to the popular guitar, got its magic sound.* Long ago, weathering cracked the case of an ordinary lute. Its sound immediately took on a new and more beautiful quality, and its fame spread quickly. Thereafter lute-makers would do anything to produce a crack in their instruments, even hitting them with rocks if necessary.

The story is also told of a skilled violin-maker who once created a large number of handsome new violins, and then traveled all across Europe trading them for old, battered violins. But he was not as crazy as some people thought, for at the conclusion of his bartering forays the craftsman ended up with a highly valued collection of Stradivarius-made violins as well as other instruments whose age and cracks gave them a tone of imcomparable beauty.

When I heard the story of this ingenious tradesman I went home immediately to check the violin my mother had left me as an heirloom. It had belonged originally to my grandfather, a prestigious violinist (in my eyes at least) who had collected and played several violins during his lifetime. And sure enough, the sought-after crack in the case was there. I recalled how, when I had first examined that violin some years before, I had actually lamented seeing the crack in the case; believing the instrument to have been damaged, I even wondered if I could find a violin-maker who would restore it to its original condition.

Every person who has an affliction has a "crack" in the "case." There may be one major crack and several minor cracks, or there may be several major cracks and minor ones as well. Frequently, though, such cracks in the case improve the quality of "sound" from the afflicted person's life.

Some people may take issue with my assumption that affliction so "weathers" the body that the person takes on a new quality of life. They may insist that too many cracks can actually produce cacophony or conflicting resonance, a garbled rather than a pure sound. However, I am drawing my conclusions from my knowledge of disabled friends and from my own experience. I have been taught as much about courage and adaptability from handicapped acquaintances as from "normal" friends.

I am not a violin-maker, but I consider myself as one of those whom Virginia Satir describes as "people-makers."* I am concerned that people actualize as much of their true potential as they are willing to do. A handicapped person, however limited by disablement, may yet realize strengths never before actualized. No one's potential for growth should be discounted. In every "case," including that of the handicapped, the human organism has a tremendous capacity for compensation and renewal.

Since the word *person* comes from the Latin *persona* or mask, which literally means "to sound through," the analogy of person and stringed instrument seems even more appropriate.† That which sounds through the person who has suffered sufficiently to have cracks in the case may take on a new quality. That person may become more sensitive to others, more attuned to their feelings.

Such maturation does not happen automatically, but the chastening effect of pain intensifies the possibility. Some people are crushed by suffering and give up hope. But others, as a result of their suffering, display a remarkable quality of life. Chastening can come from the crack in one's case.

I have used the word *chastening* in the title of this chapter in a positive sense. Webster's Dictionary says that *chasten* means "to make purer in style; refine."‡

I believe that suffering and pain may refine the human spirit, giving it a depth and quality of openness and perceptiveness which may not have been present previously. Not that we seek out pain and suffering; but we reorganize ourselves to cope with it when it comes—as come it will to most people.

The Crack in My Own Case

I have a crack in my case. Along with many others afflicted by the same handicap, I have kidney disease. I am on a kidney machine and will probably be on it for the rest of my life. I am not a good candidate for a kidney transplant. As far as statistical evidence shows, the percentages in favor of my having a successful transplant are low. Thus I am a handicapped person in that I must spend eighteen hours each week on hemodialysis. Although I read and write while I am on the machine—much of what I have written for this book was done on dialysis—I am virtually immobile six hours each day for three days each week.

After more than fifty years of living an active life, many of which included heavy involvement in athletics—I played football and basketball in high school and basketball in college—my kidney failure was especially traumatic for me. In fact, although the signs were present for several years, I considered it highly improbable that I would go the way of all kidney disease sufferers. I firmly believed that "this too will pass," as had the illnesses I had previously experienced. The probability that I would be handicapped for the remainder of my life was not acceptable to me; consequently I did not allow myself to think about it. It took a long time for me to face that prospect realistically and begin to accept it. Now I can talk knowledgeably about the process I went through in moving toward acceptance of the reality of my own handicap.

I believe that handicapped persons have much in common, whatever their affliction. Basically they feel a sense of loss. It may be the loss of some physical or mental function. Whatever the particular loss, for the sufferer in question it results in grief, and the responses to loss are grief responses.

The Affective Responses to Loss

In her classic studies of dying and death Elisabeth Kübler-Ross has observed clinically the stages through which a person goes in working through grief.* She speaks of five distinct stages: denial and isolation, which disabled persons invariably experience; anger; bargaining; depression; and, finally, acceptance.

In my own case the grief experience has contained all of these affective responses delineated by Kübler-Ross, though they have tumbled in upon each other as transitory feelings without particular form and certainly not in unvarying sequence. Accordingly I hesitate to speak of them as "stages." I prefer the phrase "interacting states in a period of gross turmoil" to indicate what I have experienced in my response to my illness and its resulting disablement. One definition of *state* is "a condition of mind or temperament."* I went through many such states; indeed, they fluctuated considerably from one to the other in the turmoil of the early phases of my own illness. The way in which the states interacted during the beginning of my treatment for kidney disease are described in the following account of what I take to be the affective responses:

(1) During an initial period of shock the person experiences numbness.

(2) A longer time of turmoil follows, during which the Kübler-Ross "stages" are manifest as conflicting feelings in dynamic interaction. There is considerable overlapping and repetition as the person experiences correlative losses attendant upon the first. For example, the loss of a bodily (kidney) function can lead to the loss of other meaningful physical and social (athletic) activities.

(3) Ultimately there arises a tension between acceptance and resistance, and this tension continues as an ongoing affective state. The person accepts the handicap, but also resists it with varying degrees of resolve to fight it. People who have the strength and feel the freedom to complain about their affliction have the best record of survival. For one thing, they exhibit a strong fighting spirit and the will to live; for another, they usually get what is needed from those upon whom they are dependent for help and support.

The Initial Response of Shock and Denial

The numbness of shock overwhelmed me at my first awareness of the real seriousness of my illness. Like many before me I went through a period of denial. Kidney machines were obviously for other people, even people I knew, but not for me! They were for the really sick people. I denied that the occasional weekends lost to incapacitating symptoms were indicators of anything more than an episode in my otherwise rather healthy existence.

My urological problem was first discovered when I was routinely examined by a medical examiner for an insurance company. He found microscopic blood cells in the urine sample. (This discovery was made more than fifteen years before I was finally to require hemodialysis in order to survive.) A few years later, a streptococcus infection in my throat settled in my kidneys. I suffered an acute inflammation of the kidneys requiring a month of complete bed rest to get back on my feet. However, I continued to show microscopic red blood cells in my urine. A number of subsequent examinations revealed that my kidneys were gradually degenerating. The doctors did a surgical biopsy which revealed that I had a kidney disease which they labeled as glomuleronephritis. I was put on a dietary dialysis, consisting of a low protein, low salt diet. My physician continued to follow carefully the ongoing laboratory studies on my blood and urine.

Throughout this time I had refused to believe that I had a serious illness. I thought the symptoms would eventually go away. Then one day I inadvertently overheard X-ray technicians discussing my condition among themselves: "Not enough healthy tissue left for proper filtration of urine"—the words fell on my ears like the voice of doom. Although I said nothing to anyone about what I had overheard, my doctor's later announcement to me that I was a candidate for a kidney machine was almost anticlimactic.

Nonetheless his words reinforced the reality ruthlessly. I now knew that either I was to live the remainder of my life utterly dependent upon a damned machine, or undergo a kidney transplant, or die. I felt numb as I heard the doctor pronounce the words: "We have no alternative."

He then carefully explained that while I was under local anesthetic the surgeon would make an incision near my wrist, go deep into my arm, get the artery and attach it to the vein. This would put arterial blood pressure into the vein on the top of my arm and enable those dialyzing me to use needles to pick up and return the blood to the vein.

By the time I had heard all of this, my head was swimming and my heart was pounding. "Is this really happening to me?" I was saying to myself.

I was not without some vague knowledge of what dialysis was all about. A few years before, I had visited a newly installed dialysis unit. I had talked briefly with several people who were on the machines. I recall being depressed at the thought of people being kept alive on a machine, sitting quietly for hours while their blood was being cleansed. I remember raising the question with myself whether I could tolerate living like that.

That question has forced itself upon me repeatedly in the years that followed as I have run through the whole gamut of affective responses to my loss. Shock and numbness gave way to a protracted period of turmoil in which all the "stages" of grief tumbled in upon one another and the feelings of acceptance and resistance struggled for supremacy.

Pastoral Care

During the initial period of shock and numbness I have been describing, the appropriate pastoral response is simply to stand by the sufferer in strength and support. The fewer the words, the better. Many of the words spoken during this time can be irritating to people, especially if the pastor attempts to communicate understanding. Persons afflicted for the first time usually feel that the experience in unique to them, that no one can truly understand what they are going through. Thus the best pastoral care is simply to be *with* the person in pain and to manifest care and concern.

Pastoral action during the ensuing time or turmoil continues to require being *with* the person in supportive strength. Additionally, however, it means to facilitate grief work, the expression of conflicting feelings concerning the loss and losses. When people finally begin to accept the reality of their handicaps the value of the pastoral relationship as sustaining care becomes important, and I will speak of this in detail in later chapters.

Esssentially the pastor helps people keep up their struggle against giving in to the handicap while at the same time encouraging them to accept it. Handicapped people also need to be reminded that their value as persons is not in what they do or how much they do but simply in their very being. This is critically important for persons living in a society which routinely interprets usefulness in terms of productivity!

Even though most new public facilities are being built today with the handicapped in mind, much architecture takes no account whatever of their specific needs. More troublesome than their treatment by society, however, are the handicapped individuals' own feelings about their particular situation. A crack in the case can be a tragic calamity or it can be a fresh new opportunity, depending largely on what the sufferer decides to feel about it and do about it. If persons' self-concepts are determined largely by their accomplishments, they will probably have great difficulty accepting the handicap. Individuals who already have strong positive feelings about themselves are likely to be transformed by the experience into warm, sensitive persons.

People engaged in pastoral care with handicapped persons will probably be understanding and effective to the degree that they can enter imaginatively into the suffering and loss of those persons: What is it like to be looked at with pity, or avoided or ignored, or led to believe that there is no place for you? Pastors need to know—and feel.

Simulating Experiences

By exercising careful observation and a cultivated imagination the pastor can simulate the disablement of any handicapped person and get at least a limited feeling for what the handicap is like. Pastors can simulate experiences by working with a partner who will help them keep from losing perspective in the experience, yet make it real enough to feel *with* handicapped people. Spoofing the simulated experience is counterproductive; it may allay the pastors' anxiety but will greatly diminish the intensity and usefulness of the experience. The following are some game-simulation experiences which the counselor can use in order to understand and feel what it is like to have a crack in the case:

—Spend enough time in a wheelchair to get a feeling of what it is like to live in one. When you get out of the chair, use crutches but don't use your legs. Be sure to have someone help you so you will also know the feeling of dependency.

—Go on a "blind walk" with someone you trust. Keep your eyes closed throughout your walk and depend entirely on your guide. Experience your environment through other senses such as hearing and touching.

—Stuff your ears with cotton and join a discussion group. Watch lips to see if you can discern what is being said. Discuss with the group your feelings about not being able to hear.

—Place yourself on the floor as though you have fallen there. Take a minute or so just to be there and to study your surroundings. Now decide what you will do in order to get the help you need.

—Sit in a chair for five or six hours without getting up. Hold steady and motionless the arm you do not ordinarily use, as though you have hypodermic needles in it which, if dislodged, would cause profuse bleeding.

—Do not talk to anyone for two days, but communicate only by means of body language or other signals. This simulates the loss of speech, aphasia, which is common to victims of stroke or other brain damage.

—Experience daily activities as an armless person. Try putting on your clothes without using your hands and arms. For more specific directions read Harold Wilke's *Using Everything You've Got.**

Pastors have a unique opportunity for entering vicariously into the experience of the sufferers they seek to help. They also have, in their faith, unique resources for making the effort.

Theological Resources

"For since he himself has passed through the test of suffering, he is able to help those who are meeting their test now" (Heb. 2:18, NEB). God's human suffering and death in the form of Jesus Christ is the supreme act of love and care.

In his book *Answer to Job* C. G. Jung avers that God discovered his own "shadow side" in relation to Job's suffering, to which God in his impassive omnipotence was obviously insensitive; Job demonstrated that he was more noble than God. "Anyone can see how he unwittingly raises Job by humiliating him in the dust. By so doing he (Yahweh) pronounces judgment on himself and gives man the moral satisfaction whose absence we found so painful in the Book of Job."* Jung feels that God became aware of his own imperviousness to human suffering and, because his nature is loving, God made the decision to enter into human suffering and death. The Incarnation is thus a sign of hope that humanity is not left alone in suffering, pain, death, grief, and loss.

Paul Tillich in *The Courage to Be* makes a similar assumption in a different way. Stating that Stoicism or neo-Stoicism has presented the only real alternative to Christianity in regard to a view of fate and death, Tillich says the Christian option is hopeful. The Stoics and their heirs emphasized "courage to be" *in spite of* the accidents and material decay that threatened being.† The Stoics were taught to live above suffering and death. As far as they are concerned, God is beyond suffering. In Christianity, however, writes Tillich: "The courage of wisdom and resignation is replaced by the courage of faith in salvation—faith in a God who paradoxically participates in human suffering. Stoicism retired into the background when faith in cosmic salvation replaced the courage of cosmic renunciation.‡

The implication of these words from Tillich is significant for anyone working with handicapped persons. Participation in their feelings enables the pastor to understand them. It also communicates to them the pastor's own humanity. The pastor who communicates empathy and humanity can be truly instrumental in facilitating the chastening process attendant upon disability, and in enriching and deepening the new tones that sound forth from the cracked case.

This is true not only in the initial stages of loss but also after a person with a new disability begins to come out of the merciful numbness of shock and regains feelings. The pastor's help extends into the protracted periods of turmoil and tension which follow.

2. Advocating Turmoil and Maintaining Tension

Ruth Ann, eighteen years old, had just finished high school and was working in an office. She had been in good health throughout her childhood and youth. One morning, shortly after she awoke, she complained to her mother that she was having trouble using her right arm. When she began experiencing paralysis of the right side of her body, her mother took her to the family physician.

The doctor at first suspected that Ruth had poliomyelitis. Tests, however, did not confirm that diagnosis. The doctor then prescribed several medications and set a time for her next appointment. Again finding no apparent basis for her condition the doctor this time concluded that she was suffering from hysterical paralysis. Her mother was advised to get her up and encourage her to do things with her unaffected left arm. However, her mother confessed that she herself could not stand to see her daughter go through the pain Ruth Ann seemed to suffer when she was out of bed.

The girl made no further effort to rise or to exercise her body. She said she was ready and willing to die; indeed, she wished to do so quickly. As it turned out, she remained in bed under constant care until her death a few years later.

Ruth Ann had accepted her illness quite early and given up with relatively little struggle against it. This was her answer to the turmoil she was experiencing during the early phases of her illness. She had resolved the tension between acceptance and resistance by giving up.

Turmoil is the confused state of the ill or injured person after the numbness of the initial shock wears off. In this state conflicting feelings rush in upon each other. The afflicted person is without purpose or direction. Feelings oscillate between accepting the illness or hurt at one time and fighting strenuously against it another time. The person is unable to become reintegrated. Ironically, shocks in life often do not come singly. A person might be able to work through a particular loss in stages, but the losses come in bunches. Thus a person may be faced with several shocks, several losses during a given period of time. In fact losses of one kind or another may precipitate others, so that the sufferer begins to feel like the victim of some trick of fate.

Advocating Turmoil

The pastor can help during this time of confused feelings and lack of direction. Such help may well take the form of what I call advocating turmoil. Advocating as a pastoral activity is actually an effort to truncate the period of painful turmoil by helping the person confront it and sort out the troubling attitudes, feelings, and behaviors. The pastor lends support and stability as needed so as to help the person begin to reorganize the self and take realistically into account the limitations imposed by the new state of affairs.

Being an advocate of the newly handicapped person means: (1) having a strong perception of what that person is experiencing; (2) getting the person into relationships with similarly handicapped people who have made adjustments, people who can not only serve as models but also be concretely supportive (I will have more to say about this in chapter 8); (3) helping the disabled persons begin to reintegrate, to actualize the personal potential for growth in spite of the newly imposed limitations; and (4) encouraging the handicapped person in achieving acceptance of the reality of the situation as well as in maintaining continued resistance to the disablement.

When I speak of truncating the turmoil I am using the word *truncate* in its literal sense. Cutting off turmoil altogether is precisely what I do *not* mean. Grief work must be allowed to occur; this is vitally important. However, cutting down the length of the turmoil period is highly desirable. Eventually handicapped persons must become mobilized to act in their own behalf. The sooner this can be accomplished, the better.

Agonizing questions invariably crop up during time of turmoil:

What can I do now? How are others going to see me? How is this going to change things for me? Why did this happen to me anyway? What did I do to deserve this? What will I still be able to enjoy and what will be denied me? Handicapped people are deeply troubled over such recurrent questions.

The five stages Elisabeth Kübler-Ross has discerned in the terminally ill—denial and isolation, anger, bargaining, depression, and acceptance—are all to be found during the period of turmoil for the handicapped. They come and go indiscriminately, appearing in random sequence and diverse combinations. Turmoil is thus like a storm at sea. The person fears being swept overboard by the waves of anger and depression. Just as the calm, sure hand of the captain at the wheel gives assurance to the occupants of a beleaguered ship, so the pastor who stands faithfully alongside as a confident pilot can help steer the disabled persons who are making the decisions and taking the steps that lead toward reorganization of their selves and their lives.

Entering the Experience of the Handicapped

And whence comes the pastor's confidence? It comes from entering into the pain and suffering of the handicapped person and learning at firsthand what that person is thinking and feeling. This is done not only through such game simulations as were suggested in chapter 1, but also through deep encounter with the thoughts, feelings, and actions of the disabled person.

Pastoring persons may at first be timid about approaching handicapped persons, but they soon learn that disabled people usually welcome—eventually if not initially—another human's basic concern for their well-being. What the handicapped resent is the condescending attitude of people who disavow the continuing potential of disabled persons. Doing things for handicapped people without first checking out whether such efforts are wanted or needed is often interpreted as condescension; it is especially irritating to persons who do not like being considered objects of pity or scorn.

Denial and Bargaining

To enter into the experience of handicapped persons is not easy. Pastors who would do so must first be aware of the tendency in all of us toward denial of the reality of the handicap. During my time of turmoil I began by denying the reality of my illness. I was frantically exchanging one negative feeling for another and throwing in a little bargaining to see if I could "get this cup of bitterness taken from me" (Luke 22:42).

From time to time thereafter I continued to deny the reality of my kidney disease, fantasizing that I was not really there on the machine, that it was actually someone else, that for me it was only a bad dream from which, momentarily, I would awake. Then the reality would hit me, and I would swing to anger. "I have too much I want to do in this brief life of mine," I would protest vehemently to myself. "I don't have time to be on this infernal machine!"

Perhaps I would experience a miracle—a common fantasy amongst us kidney diseased—in which all the blocks in the tubules of my kidneys would come unstopped and I would urinate all over the place! Thus I did my bargaining, hopeful that prayer would accomplish that much desired end.

Depression

Between such manifestations of resistance to my illness I frequently fell into periods of depression. At such times I even entertained the notion of not going on the machine again, and wondered how long I would survive if I didn't.

Anyone who has ever been on dialysis can recount the extremities they experience during the time of training for home dialysis treatment. There are infections in shunts (the tubes implanted in the arm to carry blood to the machine), clots in shunts, infiltrations of veins with needles inserted in "green" fistulas (those veins to which an artery has been attached), shock after having excess water pulled off, sudden fright when harassed mates drop a clamp instead of shutting off air with it. All sorts of hair-raising incidents make early dialysis a constant walking on the edge of fright.

The downright complexity of the dialysis machine—which seems embarrassingly simple once one has learned it—contributes to the feeling of futility and hopelessness characteristic of the initial experience of dialysis. In any event this continuous relationship with a machine seems awesome and foreboding. It is a matter of life and death. And it raises the question whether living a part of a life is better than not living at all. For the depressed the answer to that question is often in doubt, even though there is always that strange but unquenchable hope: Who knows what the future may bring in the way of remarkable, life-giving, scientific breakthroughs?

From Anger to Acceptance

By the time the initial shock of the news of my dialysis began to subside I had already entered a period of training—along with my wife who was learning to put me on the machine and take me off again and to monitor the whole process. I could describe the subsequent stage of my affective response to the whole situation in terms of anger. I was irritated, as was my wife, at the pressures put on us by those who were training us. I railed at what seemed to be their unfair expectations in regard to our progress at particular times in our training. Only later did we discover that the trainers were purposely rather "hard-nosed" in their demands upon the patients—they did not want us to give in to the limitations imposed by our illness.

As my wife and I progressed in learning how to prepare the machine, put me on, take me off, and attend the whole process, the anxiety and anger of our early training period began to diminish. We had a few emergencies, such as leaks in the artificial kidneys which required that we go through the whole process of taking me off and putting me on again. But we were beginning to develop confidence in our ability to handle the procedures necessary to home dialysis. Also we were getting a different perspective on the work of the physicians, nurses, and others dedicated to the task of hemodialysis, and a deepening appreciation of their efforts on our behalf. So anger began to give way to acceptance of the reality of the handicap and to appreciation for those who were committed to helping me face that reality.

I became acutely aware of my own mortality. At the same time though, I reasoned that those standing beside me, apparently quite healthy, had no assurance that they would outlive me. Everyone does a little dying each day through all of life. Everyone will die eventually, some early, others late, some violently and quickly, others slowly and painfully, most of us at an inopportune time. Whatever the time or mode, death is inevitable.

This acute awareness of my mortality caused me to value more dearly each day and its many experiences. I became aware of a heightened sensitivity to my environment. Sights, sounds, and smells began to take on a new quality for me. I now value human relationship more, and I see in the people about me qualities which were once obscure to me.

The best evidence that my cracked case now produces richer melodies comes from those who experience my presence and feed back to me their appreciation of the music I am now creating. I am humbly grateful for my faith in God which has sustained me through the awful confrontation of the reality of my condition, calling me out of the occasions of despondency and putting hope in my heart.

Dialysis even improved my mental functioning. I had been unaware of how much my smoldering kidney disease had been affecting my functions generally over a comparatively long period of time. One of the symptoms of kidney failure is a reduced capacity for mental functioning. Over a period of years I had become unable to remember things, and I was nonplussed by this development because all my life I had always had an excellent memory. A recently impaired ability to recall even the names of the people who worked with me and an inability to make important connections between various data I confronted each days were but symptomatic of my total mental confusion.

But that was before dialysis. After dialysis had begun, I suddenly began to experience a clarity of thought which I had been missing for several years. I was actually excited by my newfound alertness. The physical regeneration gave a tremendous boost to my will to live. I had previously regarded my losses—those I was willing to recognize—as an inevitable concomitant of growing old. It was only after being on hemodialysis for a while that I became aware of how I had previously been adapting little by little to the seemingly inevitable changes, and the degree to which I had actually been disintegrating both physically and mentally. Now I usually feel so improved in general well-being after dialysis that I welcome rather than dread it.

Walking on the razor's edge between life and death, confronting the reality of death, one invests more in life! Prior to dialysis, I often frittered time away, apparently under the illusion that I would exist interminably. Now I value time even when I do not structure it around some productive activity. I appreciate the time I take for my own enjoyment and fun. I feel less driven and more relaxed despite the imposition of the kidney machine on my free time.

Although I experience severe limitations as far as travel is concerned, I continue to attend conferences and meetings. I arrange to visit dialysis centers in the cities where such meetings are held. Thus I have not been grossly restricted even though I miss some of the sessions during the hours of my dialysis. I have learned to accept such limitations as part of the reality of my contemporary life.

Maintaining the Tension Between Acceptance and Resistance

I seem now to fluctuate between times of accepting the reality of my illness and times of resisting it strongly. When I give in to the pull toward apathy and indifference I get careless with my special diet and the regimen required for taking care of myself. Usually I pay for what carelessness with a hospitalization episode to get "straightened out" again. During the hospitalization I find that I am making resolutions to do what I know I must do in order to maintain my physical stability. It is mostly at those times that my will to fight comes to the fore and I say to myself, "I will not let this affliction get me. I will beat it one way or another!" Hence my resistance clashes with my acceptance, the two maintaining a continuing tension within me. The turmoil which characterized the dynamics of the handicapped person in the early phases of disablement is clearly followed by an ongoing tension between acceptance and resistance.

Pastoral care during the tension between acceptance and resistance can be invaluable. Its aim should be to maintain the tension, so that neither acceptance nor resistance prevails uncontested.

Such care may well include: (1) establishing a relationship or building upon one that has already been established; (2) confronting persons with their reality-denying behavior wherever that is a factor; (3) blocking attempts at irresponsible acting-out, behavior so reckless as to suggest that one were tempting death; (4) rewarding responsible behavior with approval; (5) helping persons learn to satisfy their needs in reality-oriented ways; and (6) exploring with the handicapped various possibilities for making and implementing plans for enriching and fulfilling activities in the future.

Sufferers Synonymous

One highly significant act of pastoral care with handicapped persons is to help them become aware of other persons having similar handicaps, especially if such people have developed ways of successfully reintegrating their personality and life. Drawing upon the premise which has made Alcoholics Anonymous an important support system for sufferers from alcoholism, I refer to persons manifesting handicaps of a similar nature as "sufferers synonymous," by which I mean they have a common name for their suffering. Just as the alcoholics feel the support and understanding of others who have been through "what I am suffering," persons with a handicap may be greatly encouraged by observing how another person has handled a similar handicap.

This was abundantly true in my case. One of the ways my physician briefed me for getting ready for dialysis was to tell me about a well-known attorney who had been on dialysis, at that time for more than seven years. I resolved I would visit this man and learn at firsthand how he felt and what adjustments he had made.

The attorney greeted me warmly and patiently answered every question I could think to ask him. Some questions were of an intensely personal nature. He was as open to them as to any others. I went away from that meeting in high spirits, feeling and actually saying to myself, "If he can do it, I can! I am now ready to look forward to more years of life, and make the most of it!"

This was not idle pep talk. On those occasions when I have had reversals and complications attendant to the dialysis process, I have been buoyed up by recalling that conversation and by reminding myself that that attorney continues to do well. I have kept check on his progress and it has been a continuous source of inspiration to me.

The attorney has since had a kidney transplant, which has been so successful that I have been encouraged to consider that also. His courage and faith have been an example to me. I have found that our personal exchanges enable me to face my own dialysis with greater strength.

I have since met other sufferers of kidney failure in the more than three years that I have been dialyzed. Some of these I have met in dialysis centers across the country where I have been a guest during my trips to other cities. They too have been inspiring to me and have provided a support system which is reassuring.

A Mutual Ministry

The time of turmoil and tension offers opportunities for pastoring people to "be with" handicapped people, to provide both confrontation and support as these are needed—often they are needed at one and the same time—and, above all, to learn from the intensely personal experiencing of the disabled person what effective pastoral care can be. Such pastoral care is needed with nonhandicapped persons as well, but is is especially crucial for— and illuminated by—handicapped people with particular disabilities. Pastoral care comes best out of relationships in which a mutuality of care is manifest.

Pastoral confrontation and support can be powerfully conducive to generating hope in a handicapped person. Where the pastor's advocacy helps the afflicted to face the turmoil realistically and to maintain the tension between resistance and acceptance, the revised situation can lead to a renewed sense of self-worth, and the will to live begins to reemerge.

3. Reinforcing the Will to Live

Facing the eventuality of her death from leukemia, Lois Jaffe, Associate Professor in the Graduate School of Social Work at the University of Pittsburg, wrote a beautiful and moving account of her experiencing of the "coda syndrome." Her reflection on her "slow leave-taking" from the ones she loved articulates well a goal for handicapped persons:

> To feel that one can *do* something to affect one's longevity is life-promoting. This active responsibility may take several forms, whether it is working at something one loves, participating in medical experimentation, or learning relaxation and meditation techniques to help master the tension of living a coda phase. Leaving no stone unturned in the push for longer survival, while quality of life remains, diminishes one's sense of helplessness and hopelessness.*

This young, dying woman's soul-stirring statement says it well: the important thing is to leave "no stone unturned" in the push to survive, while at the same time realizing and sustaining quality of life. This is what can diminish the sense of helplessness and hopelessness which often attends the handicapped person.

Rehabilitation

"Doing something" is also extremely important. Indeed, that is why rehabilitation centers exist. The people who work in such centers have the challenging daily task of keeping up the morale of people with gross limitations. Skilled professionals, they work with people who have been injured in accidents or have suffered catastrophic illnesses. Included among their patients are paraplegics, quadraplegics, brain-damaged individuals, and stroke victims.

In order to see and understand the efforts expended in rehabilitating such persons I visited the rehabilitation center at the Community Hospital of Indianapolis. As a guest of two psychologists employed in the program,* I learned of the patient and persistent work of nurses, occupational and physical therapists, social workers, psychologists, and others engaged in providing direct services to persons in the process of rehabilitation.

The two psychologists see each one of the patients in the rehabilitation program briefly for diagnostic and treatment purposes. They lead groups of patients in sessions which are both educative and therapeutic. Both of the psychologists stated that they are ultimately dependent upon the patient's own will to live. They must rely on the patient's personal responsiveness to the care and encouragement they offer. Most patients do respond, but some do not. The former have a good record of adaptation to rehabilitation; the latter do not rehabilitate well.

Some patients never develop the will to live. They simply give up. They succumb to despair and hopelessness, and sometimes even death. However, the psychologists marvel at the resurgence of the will to live which they observe in most patients. Patients with a strong will to live cooperate painstakingly with the people seeking to help them. Indeed, this is one of the great satisfactions of those at the center who are doing the rehabilitative work.

The two psychologists pointed out that those patients who have a strong and vital religious faith seem also to do best in recapturing the will to live. Although the doctors had not studied this phenomenon particularly, they reflected upon their own experience with such patients and arrived at a consensus on the importance of the religious factor. At least, they declared, patients who have the resources of their faith to draw upon tend to be more hopeful than those who do not.

The patients' will to live is augmented by their successes in step-by-step reintegration of their personality organization. As compensatory bodily functions are developed, hope for such total reorganization increases and the will to live is correspondingly strengthened. In the largest percentage of cases new goals for behavior and living are established and the patient's total morale is improved.

Behavior Modification as Reinforcement

Behavior modification is one of the methods used today for rehabilitating patients with serious handicaps. The method calls

for reinforcement of particular constructive behaviors which get
the patient on the way to recovery. This reinforcement is accomplished through rewarding the patient for such constructive
behavior and denying the patient the opportunity to engage in
behavior that may be destructive to self or others.

Mrs. Williams, an accident victim, took an extraordinary
amount of time to eat her food because she was continually talking with other patients. Much of the time she did this to the
detriment of her own nutritional needs—she tended not to finish
her meals. Finally the psychologists recommended that she be
isolated from the other patients while taking her meals. Then
she was rewarded for completing her meal by being placed once
again among the other patients so she could resume her conversations with them. Eventually by such isolation and return Mrs.
Williams was weaned away from her destructive pattern. She
was able to establish control of her talking while eating sufficiently to get her own proper nourishment.

I do not recommend that pastors engage in such authoritative
methods of behavior modification. What pastors can do is to give
positive "strokes" to people who are acting in ways that are constructive to themselves and others. Positive strokes may be
given in the form of words of encouragement and approval.
They may also take the form of reassuring touch. In fact the
very time and attention the pastor gives to handicapped people
are in themselves positive strokes, especially if they are given in
an attitude of genuine caring.

The pastor should not attempt to "rescue" handicapped persons but instead trust the basic will to live as it reemerges. When
I rescue a drowning man I do something for him that I believe
he cannot do for himself. Any attempt to "rescue" the handicapped really communicates a basic lack of faith in that person's
capacity to grow. It reinforces the impression of the handicapped
person as victim, unable to assume help by learning personal
responsibility.

Pastors and congregations can help by learning what are the
particular interests of a disabled person, and then cater to those
interests when they see the person cooperating with the workers
in the rehabilitation process. For example, if the person likes to
read, the gift or loan of books will be a reinforcement of positive

behavior. Nurturing and rewarding the consuming interests of the handicapped person can constructively contribute in an essential way to the reinforcement process.

Motivating Groups

Support systems of many sorts exist for a variety of purposes. In the case of the handicapped, supportive therapy groups can provide a powerful reinforcement of the will to live.

Mr. Allen is an extremely bright thirty-two-year-old machinist whose potentially brilliant career was threatened by a tragic accident. His usual pattern of behavior was to rise at about daybreak and get his exercise by walking the family's dog. Then he would eat his breakfast and go early to his work at a local manufacturing concern.

On this particular summer day Mr. Allen rose early as usual and took the dog out for the customary walk. As he was moving along the berm of the road a car swerved wildly and struck him, knocking him into the ditch at the side of the road. There he lay, injured, as the car sped away from the scene of the accident. His trusted dog remained loyally by his side.

Fortunately a newsboy carrying his papers in the vicinity about an hour later saw the victim lying in the ditch. Although the dog kept him from getting close, the boy thought he recognized the victim as Mr. Allen, one of his customers. He went home immediately and had his mother call for help.

Mr. Allen recovered consciousness at the hospital. Through X-rays and other diagnostic procedures, the doctors determined that he had received some brain damage. His speech was not affected by the brain damage, but some of his functions were. When he became aware of his condition Mr. Allen expressed the wish to die. He refused to cooperate with the doctors. He was sent to the rehabilitation center where he met the psychologists who were assigned to work with him. At first he refused to see them or talk with them.

The psychologists explained to Mr. Allen that with retraining of his muscles he undoubtedly could become responsible for himself. He did not seem to want to hear and withdrew from other patients who tried to relate to him.

As soon as he began to heal physically, Mr. Allen was placed in a group. Other quadraplegics provided a model for him. He began to be encouraged about his own possibilities. The psychologists suggested specific goals for his behavior and rewarded him with positive feedback for each one he achieved. After a few individual sessions with the psychologists, and with the tremendous support system provided by the group, Mr. Allen began to develop his will to live. His relationship with a female occupational therapist contributed greatly to that process. He liked her and desired to please her by accomplishing what she asked him to do. The quality of these relationships in the rehabilitation process was great and undoubtedly contributed much to Mr. Allen's desire to recover and his acceptance of the limitations under which he must now live. He has discovered, and tends to rely more on, what he can do for himself.

I saw Mr. Allen after he had been in the rehabilitation process for more than a year. I found him cheerful, enthusiastic, and helpful in working with other patients. He now challenges the other patients to achieve their goals and to strengthen their will to live. He makes an excellent model for them because he understands the total experience of sudden loss of function and its emotional concomitants.

Religious Resources

Reinforcement of the will to live can occur through the therapy group. It can also be augmented through the use of religious resources. Scripture, prayer, and devotional readings can be used by the pastor with great effectiveness, especially if they flow quite naturally out of spiritual integrity. If they are presumed to have some magical efficacy in themselves apart from a pastoral relationship, their use can actually be an affront to the handicapped person instead of a call to spiritual formation. The use of religious resources within a pastoral relationship can be a tremendous source of inspiration to the handicapped person.

The pastor can conclude a visit with prayer or leave with the handicapped person devotional literature to read later as may seem desirable. Or the pastor may read appropriate portions of Scripture, inspirational poetry, or other insightful passages. Examples of such material abound:

If we can love—this is the touchstone—if we can bring people about whom we are concerned to the place where they are able to receive love and to offer love, then healing will have taken place.

—Karl Menninger (paraphrase)*

Verily I say unto you, inasmuch as ye have done it unto one of the least of these, my brethren, ye have done it unto me.

—Matt. 25:40

You give but little when you give of your possessions. It is when you give of yourself that you truly give."

—Kahlil Gibran†

I was eyes to the blind,/Feet to the lame;/I was a father to the needy,/And I took up the stranger's cause.

—Job 29:15–16, NEB

For it is in giving that we receive.

—St. Francis of Assisi

Humanitarianism is a link that binds together all America . . . generosity has never impoverished the giver; it has enriched the lives of those who have practiced it . . . and the bread that we have cast upon the waters has been returned in blessings a hundredfold.

—Dwight D. Eisenhower‡

The best portion of a good man's life,/His little nameless, unremembered acts of kindness and love.

—William Wordsworth§

For truly, I say to you, if you have faith as a grain of mustard seed, you will say to this mountain, "Move hence to yonder place, and it will move; and nothing will be impossible to you.

—Matt. 17:20–21

And to keep me from being unduly elated by the magnificence of such revelations, I was given a sharp pain in my body which came as Satan's messenger to bruise me; this was to save one from being unduly elated. Three times I begged the Lord to rid me of it, but his answer was: "My grace is all you need; power comes to its fullest strength in weakness."

—2 Cor. 12:7–8, NEB

And Jesus answered them, "Go and tell John what you hear and see: the blind receive their sight and the lame walk, lepers are cleansed and the deaf hear, and the dead are raised up, and the poor have good news preached to them."

—Matt. 11:4–5

Strengthen the weak hands, and make firm the feeble knees. Say to those who are of a fearful heart, Be strong, fear not!

Behold, your God will come with vengeance, With the recompense of God. He will come and save you! Then the eyes of the blind shall be opened and the ears of the deaf unstopped; Then shall the lame man leap like a hart! And the tongue of the dumb sing for joy.

—Isa. 35:3–6

A man is only complete when he has a true friend to understand him, to share all his passions and sorrows with, and to stand by him throughout his life.*

The quality of life to which we aspire and the questioning at home and abroad of our commitment to the democratic ideal make it imperative that our nation utilize to the fullest the potential of all citizens.

—President's Task Force on Women's Rights and
Responsibilities, December 16, 1969

The beginning of a devotional attitude, then, may properly be seen as humility. . . . The second step in our devotional pilgrimage is a full acceptance of God's salvation and grace. . . . Grace is the ability to be grateful for what God has left us in spite of what the physical handicap has taken away—in spite of all the problems, illnesses, difficulties, and losses. . . . The last step in our devotional journey—or perhaps the first one we take after we have returned from the presence of God—is that of an understanding and love of people.†

Quotations such as these may be copied on cards or reproduced in other ways and left with the handicapped person, to be referred to when the need for such encouragement is felt.

Open, honest, genuine, relaxed transactions between pastoring people and disabled people greatly enrich both. Hope and courage are mutually engendered. The handicapped person's will to live can be greatly reinforced by the love and acceptance of a pastoring person. Likewise, courage in the face of pain and suffering contain powerful lessons for pastoring people who are not handicapped.

Handicapped persons' efforts toward their own rehabilitation get strongly motivated when they are keenly aware of a caring and supportive community. It is part of the pastoral approach to manifest and to nurture such caring and support, and generally to foster the push toward wholeness made by the disabled persons themselves.

4. Motivating the Push toward Wholeness

A brilliant young paraplegic physician, whose grave injury derived from an automobile accident, recently said to me,

> Once I was able to get my feelings expressed and straighten out my attitudes toward my disability and myself generally, I was ready to resume my practice. At that point I had to decide precisely what I was going to do now to arrange my examining room in a way that would meet my needs—I would have to have all necessary instruments within easy reach. During those early attempts at adapting myself to my handicap I was frustrated many times, but I soon found that I could effectively organize my environment to fit my new requirements. I now practice medicine about as proficiently as I ever did.

Rehabilitation requires dealing simultaneously with feelings and behaviors. "What am I going to do?" becomes the emergent question once the feelings of anger and depression have been dealt with. "What concrete steps are necessary for me now to get myself going again, so I can be as productive as possible?" For the disabled person these questions establish the challenge to action.

Total Reorganization

The action is toward total reorganization of the self in terms of attitudes and behaviors appropriate to the handicapped situation. It requires a total reorganization because, as in the case of the nonhandicapped as well, one's attitude toward oneself determines to a great degree how that person will function vocationally and in most other areas of life.

The Thrust toward Wholeness

A truly informed and caring pastor is aware of the powerful thrust toward health and wholeness which is already at work in the handicapped person. Whatever trauma has occurred, whatever has occasioned the particular handicap has meant one major change for the handicapped person: it has changed a once familiar, congenial, and reliable body into a nightmare of a problem that must be dealt with. Nonetheless the inherent biological, psychological, and social drives are still there, still pushing in the direction of maintaining and enhancing the person as a whole being. Although this inherent thrust toward wholeness in every person is never automatic, it is persistent and real. The pastor's hope is that for the handicapped person this active drive will continue. Once attitudes and feelings have been dealt with, the person is usually ready to take steps to reorganize as a functioning being.

Integration in Human Being

In a classic study of the adaptive capacities of the body Walter B. Cannon marvelled at the body's wisdom: "The ability of living beings to maintain their own constancy has long impressed biologists."* Setting forth the concept of homeostasis (the body's self-regulating tendency toward constancy), Cannon perceived that the body maintains its own equilibrium.

On the other hand, biologists such as Ludwig Von Bertalanffy have recently attacked the view of homeostasis, stating instead that the living person is a unique organization or system. "Every living organism is essentially an open system," says Von Bertalanffy. "It maintains itself in a continuous inflow and outflow, a building up and breaking down of components, never being, so long as it is alive, in a state of chemical and thermodynamic equilibrium, but maintained in a so-called steady state which is distinct from the latter."†

An "open system" is one that is continually taking in nutrients, water for example, assimilating them, and making them a part of one's own total organism. The human body, as an example, takes in water, food, and ideas; it assimilates and stores them in the body for future use, and rejects or ejects as refuse whatever is unassimilated as not being useful to the body. I appreciate very much this recent emphasis on the human person as an open system because recent studies and my own experience suggest that people are not simply concerned to have equilibrium. They seek and even welcome tension in order to achieve desirable goals. Nevertheless they operate as a total organization.

Any handicap is a threat to the person as a whole. An accident to the body which results in a handicap for the person produces a total crisis. The person feels wholly threatened. When certain dramatic changes in bodily functions occur, people feel, whether they are teenagers or older persons, that their whole being is in danger.

In puberty, for example, the body, which was once quite stable, begins to change in form and function. Girls' breasts begin to develop and menstruation begins. Boys develop pubic hair and their voices begin to deepen. Endocrinal changes upset the familiar rhythms. Adolescents experience so many changes in the once reliable body that they often become shy, awkward, and embarrassed by what they are becoming. Although they may be well informed about what is happening to them physically, the whole transformation is a new and different experience with which they must also learn to cope emotionally. All of this often produces a crisis in their personality.

Similarly, physical changes occurring in later years upset the once relatively reliable bodily organization. Degenerative illnesses, one of the most common being arteriosclerosis, diminish the person's capacity to function. The result may well be a personality crisis that requires far-ranging adjustments.

Personal Crisis

A threat to any part of the body is usually perceived as a threat to the whole person. The comprehensive experiencing of such a threat triggers anxiety. In *The Meaning of Anxiety* Rollo May states: "Anxiety is the apprehension cued off by a threat to some value which the individual holds essential to his existence as a personality."* Loss of some function poses a threat. It may involve the loss of some member of the body such as the arms or legs, or the loss of movement attendant upon paralysis of the body, or loss of physical functions, impairment of organs, loss of sensory capacities. Any of these losses may pose a threat to the whole personality, thereby producing a crisis in the person.

This crisis in the person, as we have seen, can be an opportunity for growth. Whether it becomes that or not depends largely on the attitude afflicted persons adopt toward themselves: "Can I arrive at a positive view of myself as a whole person, and silence the voice of terror that screams from the loss itself, "You are less than whole and never will be whole again!"

The possibility that the individual will again value himself or herself as a whole person is a real possibility. It is also possible to help people who are into the process of reorganizing themselves as whole persons despite the loss.

Stimulating the Growth Potential

Several years ago Abraham H. Maslow perceived that studies of personality had been done largely in institutions populated with patients who represented aberrations from "normal" functioning.* He deemed such studies misleading, especially if they were judged to be setting forth norms for determining the nature of the person. Maslow therefore set out to do research with normal persons. He concluded from his studies that people in general have a hierarchy of needs, and once these needs are filled, people move on toward actualizing their potential for growth. Thus Maslow saw the "growth motive" as a powerful thrust within persons: "Growth takes place when the next step forward is subjectively more delightful, more joyous, more intrinsically satisfying than the last; the only way we can ever know what is right for us is that it feels better subjectively than any alternative. The new experience validates itself rather than being validated by any outside criterion."†

The Struggle to Grow

Maslow goes on to say that two forces are continually at war within us. One, with an eye on safety, is pulling us back into defensiveness and nonrisking behavior; the other, with an eye on growth, is pushing us toward independence and freedom. This generalization is especially true when considerable trauma has been experienced in connection with whatever caused a particular handicap. Maslow diagrams these antithetical forces in a way that is suggestive of how they may frame the options for the person affected: *

Enhances the dangers   Enhances the attractions

SAFETY ◄——— Person ———► GROWTH

Minimizes the attractions   Minimizes the dangers

Once the disabled people have dealt with their feelings of denial and anger, they are usually ready to get the satisfactions that come with retraining their muscles or exercising their bodies in rehabilitation—and to minimize the dangers that attend the process. Thus individuals are likely to be open to their growth potential within the limitations imposed by the handicap.

On the other hand, if handicapped people become preoccupied with the dangers—fear of failure or being hurt, embarrassment at falling or fumbling in some way—thus minimizing the "attractions," the accomplishment of even simple tasks will be difficult. They are likely to "play it safe" and perhaps refuse even to cooperate in their own rehabilitation.

Healthy growth is:

> . . . a never ending series of free-choice situations confronting each individual at every point throughout his life, in which he must choose between the delights of safety and growth, dependence and independence, regression and progression, immaturity and maturity. Safety has both anxieties and delights; growth has anxieties and delights. We grow forward when the delights of growth and the anxieties of safety are greater than the anxieties of growth and the delights of safety.†

Growth in the Handicapped

The reality of this phenomenon of growth is seen with particular clarity in the situation of some handicapped people. Rather than face the embarrassment of defeat, a person may withdraw to safety and become defensive about the handicap.‡

Growth occurs when the person takes the first few steps toward rehabilitation. Seeing the success of others with similar handicaps, the person may be encouraged greatly to believe in the possibility of success. Knowing someone who has overcome a similar handicap and is functioning well has the effect of maximizing the attractions and stimulating the potential for growth.

Power and Weakness

Our weaknesses are present opportunities for growth. Through our weaknesses we become aware of the need for exercising aspects of our being which might otherwise go unnoticed and unattended. This phenomenon is frequently referred to as compensation.

Compensation

The body usually compensates for losses of functions. When one part of the body fails, some other part takes over its function and thereby becomes strengthened. If one eye is lost, the other becomes stronger. Loss of arms leads to the development of new skills in the use of feet and legs. One of the strongest men I know has a powerfully developed upper torso, massive arms and shoulders; and he is not a gymnast but only a weight lifter of sorts—he lifts himself and his paralyzed legs around all day on crutches!

The Apostle Paul, in his Second Letter to the Corinthians, speaks of his own experience in this regard:

> And so to keep me from being unduly elated by the magnificence of such revelations, I was given a sharp pain in my body which came as Satan's messenger to bruise me; this was to save me from being unduly elated. Three times I begged the Lord to rid me of it, but his answer was: "My grace is all you need; power comes to its full strength in weakness." Hence, I am well content for Christ's sake, with weakness, contempt, persecution, hardship, and frustration; for when I am weak, then I am strong (2 Cor. 12:7–10, NEB).

Demosthenes, the Greek patriot, had handicaps that would have been extremely discouraging to most young men. His voice was harsh and unpleasant—"unmusical," or so his biographer wrote of him.* His lungs were weak, so he did not have resonance. Furthermore he was described as an awkward person.

Through rigid self-discipline Demosthenes trained himself for public speaking. The story is told that he recited verses as he climbed the steep hills of his homeland. And as he climbed he projected his voice against the roar of the sea, even placing pebbles in his mouth to improve his diction. In many ways he prepared himself for the important public role he was to play. Demosthenes became one of the great orators of ancient Greece. His weakness became his strength.

Organism and Total Organization

Kurt Goldstein, working with brain-damaged individuals, marvelled at their wondrous capacities to adapt.* Where the affliction had affected one part of the organism another part took up the slack. Goldstein's observations led him to conclude that the human being is an integrated organism and that the organism functions out of its total organization.

> All events in the organism, even though they may take place in parts, are holistic. The more they take place in isolated parts, the more mechanistic they become, and the more they become like "physical Gestalten" . . . The reason for this is that they occur in parts which are relatively isolated from the whole, and which are embedded in a relatively stable and constant topography (the rest of the organism).†

Elsewhere in the same study Goldstein observes:

> "The patient becomes well in spite of residual defect, because he replaces the lost performances by others. This idea is based on the presupposition that deficiency in function of one part can be compensated by increased function of other parts."‡

The compensating factors in the brain-damaged persons with whom Goldstein worked were powerful indeed. One could conclude that the thrust toward wholeness operating in such individuals was extremely potent. The tendency toward total reorganization of the personal system was strong.

I have been saying throughout that there is a positive thrust toward wholeness in every person. If damage occurs to some part of the organism, the whole is affected. As a result powerful compensatory factors go into operation so that other parts of the organism become more highly developed. Thus reorganization of the personality takes place, and it is a total reorganization. This phenomenon happens emotionally as well as physically. Becoming aware of one's emotional weakness enables one to gain emotional strength. Rehabilitation of the handicapped depends upon this reorganization, which comes from the will to live.

The Pastoral Response to the
Rush Toward Wholeness

The person's will to live, as we have seen, is greatly enhanced by one's faith. Ministers of the faith can help strengthen that will to live. The pastor who is really "with" handicapped persons is also in a position to help them at many points along the path of rehabilitation, which involves a comprehensive effort at total reorganization. And the pastoral help need not stop there.

Care of the Chronically Ill

Much of what we have said clearly presupposes and stresses the importance of pastoral response to people in crisis. What happens though, one may rightfully ask, when the crisis phase of an illness or accident has passed? Often the chronically ill person gets neglected. Yet chronically ill people unquestionably need and usually welcome continuing pastoral care and support.

Surely one need is for chronically ill persons to be able to express what they are feeling about their present experience. As a chronically ill kidney patient I am keenly aware that during the early days of my illness I was getting much attention from my friends and colleagues. Now I assume they have become relatively accustomed to my acceptance of my illness, because only a few show concern for me. I do not fault them for this; indeed, I prefer that they see me as doing well because actually I am doing quite well. I am not being critical of them when I say there are times when I also have the need, however, to express what I am feeling today about the contemporary effects of my illness.

Pastoral Concerns

What are the pastoral care approaches which will contribute to the push toward wholeness? How can pastors and counselors abet this whole self-reorganization process? Two suggestions seem especially important:

(1) If people's illnesses or handicaps are detrimental to their being reemployed in their former job, help them to reassess their capabilities and to search for a new job. The slogan "Hire the handicapped" is a reminder to prospective employers that dis-

abled persons can be of inestimable value to them, especially if such persons have retrained themselves for the particular work involved. Indeed, retraining is usually a part of the rehabilitation process in a center for rehabilitation.

(2) Help the disabled develop relationships which will be sustaining and supportive to them not just vocationally but in many other ways as well. (We will say more about this in the chapters that follow.)

There are many areas of life in which periodic checking by the pastor, coupled with effective utilization of spiritual resources and involvement of the caring community, can prove helpful. Not to be overlooked is the critical area of human sexuality.

5. Supporting the Sexuality of Handicapped Persons

Sexual adequacy is exceedingly important for a positive self-concept. For the handicapped the problem of sexual adequacy is compounded by societal attitudes towards them. They are often regarded as sexless individuals: pity the poor hapless people who cannot enjoy sex. Usually though, the subject is not even mentioned in the presence of handicapped persons for fear of offending them. The general assumption seems to be that handicapped persons have lost all capacity for feeling and perhaps have even lost interest. But this is far from the truth!

Sexuality and the Handicapped

To be sure, some severely handicapped people may have lost feeling in the genital area, which is presumed to be the center of sexual activities. (Actually, in a general or nontechnical sense the brain is the center of sexual experiencing, and only when your brain is gone have you lost the capacity for sex.) However, such people can readily compensate for the loss of genital feeling. They have other areas of feeling that can be stimulated so that sexual expressions of love and care can be as available to the handicapped as to nondisabled persons. "Human sex is widely versatile," says Alex Comfort, "and not limited to the genitalia."*

Furthermore there are very few handicapped persons who are so disabled that they cannot function sexually. Hence the first requirement for most disabled persons is simply to get the facts straight concerning the implications of their handicap for their sexuality, affirm their right to be sexual, and then learn how in their own particular case sexual functioning is possible.

Allaying Anxieties

Frightening questions about sexual adequacy often occur to the person who has recently become handicapped: What has happened to my capacity for a sexual functioning? Will I no longer be a man? a woman? How will this affect my relationships? my marriage?

While I was in training for dialysis I was discussing my situation with a friend who is chaplain of a hospital in my city. He indicated that he was quite familiar with patient reaction to dialysis, since he had visited the hemodialysis unit regularly. During the course of the conversation he chanced to remark that patients often became impotent after dialysis. That remark set off an alarm signal deep inside me and I began to get anxious about becoming impotent as a consequence of my dialysis.

I resolved to see my attorney friend immediately. Knowing he had been on dialysis for more than seven years, I felt sure he would know something about the subject, and I certainly did not wish to continue worrying about what I hoped was nothing but a confused shred of information. I was greatly relieved to learn from my friend that he was potent! I was then able to say to myself what I had said so often about my dialysis in comparing it with his, though this time I said it with a wry grin, "If it will work for him it will work for me too!"

Actually, over the three-year period of my own dialysis I have occasionally experienced diminished libido on the days of dialysis, but then I have also occasionally experienced a resurgence of potency on the "off days." The fact is that my handicap has had no serious consequences for my libidinal drives, and that sexual adequacy has not become a prime cause for anxiety.

Affirming Sexuality

Not much has been written to lift the level of popular knowledge about how persons with handicaps can and do function sexually. Literature on the subject can often be gleaned only by a laborious search among the books and professional journals in medical libraries. And most of that is in such technical jargon that it is not readily available to the handicapped patients themselves.

One sensitive and frank little book on the subject finally appeared under the title *Sexual Options for Paraplegics and Quadraplegics.* It is a responsible, open, honest, and pictorially illustrated book. Written by Thomas O. Mooney, Theodore M. Cole, and Richard A. Chilgren, with a foreword by Alex Comfort, its authors sanction the disabled person's "right to be sexual":*

> Until recently, few people have openly encouraged the physically disabled to use their bodies to satisfy themselves and please their partners. We endorse sexual expression for its ability to enhance personal pleasure, improve communication, and build self-esteem. *This is especially important for those who have shunned open exchange about sexual capabilities because of self-consciousness, disability, and embarrassment.* For some, endorsement may be the first step out of the isolation imposed on them by the able-bodied societal norms. For others, a major obstacle to reengaging the world in a meaningful or competitive fashion is the energy drain of feeling castrated because they are sexually inept.†

In the United States alone there are more than 120,000 paraplegics and quadraplegics.‡ Most of them trace their condition to injuries of the spinal cord. Some of them wear medical devices, such as catheters and other paraphernalia, which make sexual activity difficult for them and even embarrassing to them. Four out of five spinal cord injuries are to males,§ perhaps because of the risks men run on potentially dangerous jobs or because of their aggressive behavior in potentially risky situations. For such injured males, the attendant feelings of sexual inadequacy come as a tremendous blow to masculine self-esteem. "The energy drain of feeling castrated adversely affects motivation for relating, or even the will to live."‖ Yet in most cases these disabled males, if they affirm their sexuality, can adapt to their particular disablement and still realize sexual fulfillment. Their task, of course, is to learn how to do that in their own particular circumstances.

Functioning for Fulfillment

In the preface to their book Mooney, Cole, and Chilgren state: "If sexual confidence can be reestablished, some will feel that they can now invest their energies in reentering the world of vocation, self-respect, and responsibility."# Such confidence increases as persons learn specifically how to adapt. Handicapped persons can in fact adapt to their own disability in such a way as to achieve sexual fulfillment. They may need and welcome support and guidance in doing this.

Although each person will have to discover for himself or herself how to function sexually with the particular disability, some general suggestions are possible:

(1) Disabled persons who have lost feeling in the genital area can transfer stimulation to other areas of the body where feeling is still possible. The term *alternate sensation* is used to refer to this substitute for a sensation which has been lost. Intense and satisfying feelings are possible when sensation in one part of the body is substituted for the lack of sensation in another part of the body. Experimentation will show which of the various possible substitute areas of the body provide the most gratification in feeling response.

(2) The so-called mental orgasm, which is a remembered or fantasized experience, can be as fulfilling to the disabled person as actual climaxing is to the nondisabled person. The term has reference to a state of mind really, and is the outcome of an active imagination coupled with strong, positive feelings toward one's partner. It may be helpful to consult the literature for specific guidance on how this can be done.

(3) Open and honest discussions with the partner on a continuing basis are advised. People help each other by talking about the difficulties involved in adapting to whatever medical devices are constantly required in connection with the disablement. Feelings of embarrassment, or any other feelings that may impede the relationship with one's partner can be frankly shared with the partner. Indeed, such sharing may be essential to overcoming any blocks to sexual functioning.

(4) One needs to be concerned about achieving whatever cleanliness is required to make the aesthetic appeal of the sexual relationship as attractive as possible to the partner. Especially when catheters of various kinds are required by the disabled person, careful cleaning of the body is important. The disabled person wishes to make the best possible presentation of himself or herself to the other person.

(5) Some handicapped people engage in "sensory amplification" to achieve the most pleasure and satisfaction from their sexual partners. Sensory amplification is the act of thinking about a pleasurable experience, concentrating on it, and in your mind amplifying the sensation to an intense degree.* The method is useful for bringing one's feelings to a high degree of intensity. It can even help in the achievement of the "mental orgasm" we mentioned a moment ago.

Pastoral Possibilities

Although pastors are probably not qualified to give advice regarding the medical implications of sexual activities, they can encourage the handicapped person to be aware of each individual's right to be sexual. Beyond that, pastors who are informed as to the possibilities of sexual adjustment on the part of handicapped persons can provide specific assistance.

Specific Suggestions

Pastors can encourage, support, suggest, and facilitate along certain lines. They can prompt persons to:

(1) Read articles or books on the subject. *Sexual Options for Paraplegics and Quadraplegics* would be a good recommendation. Although literature in the field is scanty and hard to come by, handicapped persons can find materials on the theme of sexual alternatives for disabled people. A group at the University of Minnesota Medical School has done extensive research on sexuality and the physically handicapped person. Theodore M. Cole and his associates have published a number of articles growing out of studies done with disabled people.†

(2) Consult physicians. The handicapped can ask their doctor quite forthrightly about specific limitations they may have in sexual functioning and how possibly to overcome them. What dangers, if any, may they encounter in sexual activity? What are ways in which they may receive help, if needed?

(3) Talk with partners. Pastors can suggest and even help to facilitate straightforward talk between partners about both the risks and the possibilities that now attend their sexual relationship. Handicapped persons who can bring themselves and their partners to such open discussion have the opportunity to

reassure their partners that they continue to be sexual beings: they are only handicapped, not desexed.

(4) Organize a group. Handicapped persons can get together, perhaps in or under the sponsorship of the church. A group or series of groups may function as a support system wherein others with similar sexual problems can exchange ideas and feelings. Supportive sharing can facilitate the process whereby each disabled person discovers how he or she can function sexually.

An Example

A group can have a dramatic effect on the disabled person's acceptance of himself or herself as a sexual being. I think in this connection of an experience I actually had with a young male student of our seminary whom I shall call Bud:

At the opening of the fall semester several years ago a bright young man on crutches appeared in my class on Personality and Christian Faith. He was propelling himself with ease even though his legs were undeveloped and immobile.

I was to learn later that as a child Bud had been stricken with poliomyelitis. While seriously ill he engaged in a mighty struggle just to survive. When he recovered he was left with both legs paralyzed. He faced life as a paraplegic. After this alert, cheerful man had completed a distinguished college career, his indomitable spirit carried him into graduate work at our seminary where he had already completed one year's work.

Bud had demonstrated that he was an able scholar, but he admitted that he concentrated so heavily on his studies in order at least in part to avoid the pain involved in searching for intimate relationships, especially with women. "How could a woman really be interested in me?" he often asked in a kind of rhetorical manner. He seemed so sure of the expected answer that he hardly waited for anyone to respond. Thus, although he did not desire to give up on any outside chance of having an intimate relationship with a woman, he seemed resigned to accept the unlikelihood of its happening.

As a part of the class organization we met in small groups. Bud's group consisted of eight students, four of whom were women. Over the course of several group sessions Bud spoke plainly of how he saw himself: since he felt that women could not be interested in him, he tended not to accept positive "strokes" from them. In fact he did not trust them.

"How do you think women in this group feel about you?" I asked.

"I don't know," he replied grimly.

"Why don't you ask them?" I countered.

"Oh, they will probably tell me I am OK, but I can't be sure whether they are pitying me or saying what they really feel," he went on.

"Don't discount them," I said firmly. "Let them speak for themselves!"

"All right, I will ask them," he responded. Then he turned to each of the women, asking how he came across to her.

Each in turn reassured him that although he impressed her as being a remarkable person she was hardly aware of his disability; and she didn't like his tendency to put them all down. He was obviously surprised and chastened by the feedback he was getting. At the end of the session he spontaneously expressed to the group how greatly affirmed he had felt during the transactions with the women in the group.

It seems almost contrived to say that within a few weeks Bud was dating a very attractive woman student of the seminary, but that is precisely what happened. Within a short time they became engaged, and during the following summer they were married. When a baby daughter was born to them Bud proudly announced her arrival to everyone he met.

Bud visited me recently and said, "You gave me permission to be sexual. I am eternally grateful to you for that." I felt great satisfaction, as the group leader, for my modest role in triggering his assertiveness as a sexual person. My confrontation and support apparently was important in pushing Bud out of the slough of nonsexual behavior and onto the solid ground of an intimate relationship which he in his "heart of hearts" really wanted!

The Sensitive Pastor

I have presented this frank introductory discussion of the sexual possibilities for persons with handicaps because I know from the personal experience of my own dialysis what a shock it can be to discover an abrupt change in sexual capacity. I have been greatly reassured by feedback from others in my situation. Such reassurance is possible for all disabled persons who will be sufficiently open to discuss the subject, especially with other disabled people whose disabilities are much like their own.

The sensitive pastor can promote the communication process by also being direct, open, and pastoral in approach. This means checking out with the disabled person how he or she feels about his or her own sexuality. If in this area there seems to be a problem, the pastor can gently draw the person out in order to determine what kinds of reassurance are needed. Gentleness and wisdom are called for as pastors approach this area of intimacy so vital to the growth and wholeness of the self.

Sexual communion is an act of love, and celebration of that love. It is truly fulfilling in the context of an intimate relationship. Relationship, intimacy, love—these are human needs of all people. Handicapped persons have not ceased, by virtue of their handicaps, to be persons. A sensitive pastor can often lead in helping them—and the people about them—to become and remain aware of that fact. Indeed, pastors have a unique opportunity to inform and serve entire families.

6. Supporting Parents of Handicapped Children

"Just tell me my baby is all right," the anxious new mother said to the man beside her bed. The doctor, who had just assisted in delivering her son, replied frankly, "I wish I could." His face and the tone of his voice communicated both sympathy and fatigue. He touched her hand and continued, "He has a curved spine. We will do everything we can to help him." She broke into tears. Holding her hand gently, the doctor said quietly, "I am sorry."

An Anguished Situation

Many times I have experienced the pain and frustration of parents in anguish over the disabilities of their children. What does one say to heartbroken people? What can one do that will be effective? What attitude does one take? What ministry can one possibly provide that will really be of help and support to them?

Mixed Emotions

Parents of handicapped children are torn by mixed emotions. They feel guilt, anger, frustration, and despair. Indeed, they run the whole gamut of emotions associated with grief and loss. They also go through a process similar to that of the handicapped themselves, a process, as I have already indicated, that is not necessarily characterized by well-defined stages. Any of these various affective states can be experienced at any time by parents of handicapped children, depending on the nature of the situation which calls out a response from them.

Most of the parents I interviewed denied feeling anger: they were not at all angry at their handicapped children, themselves, the people serving them, or anyone else. They did acknowledge various feelings of guilt, frustration, and despair, especially guilt.

Loss of Freedom

There is an impressive unanimity among parents of handicapped children with respect to one feeling. They all seem to feel deeply responsible for their disabled children and greatly circumscribed by the duties attendant upon caring for them.

Sometimes they are perplexed about how much time and attention they should be giving that task. They want to act responsibly, but handicapped children often impose heavy demands. "How far must we go?" parents ask. One mother admitted: "It is tough to tell the difference between my being frustrated with my child and my just being tired of being tied to her all the time." Parents who feel they have no time to themselves are indeed hard pressed.

A United Church of Christ minister and his wife are the parents of an autistic child whom we shall call Molly. They are close friends of mine. Indeed, my family has been associated with their family in various activities for a number of years. Their two older children, a boy and a girl, are in their late teens and in college. We have watched our families grow up together. Our recent conversations have concerned their feelings over the years since the birth of their autistic child.

They told me that their major problems had to do with feeling circumscribed by the responsibilities they feel strongly in relation to Molly. The mother said she herself felt a "total loss of freedom," especially as she compared herself to other mothers of children the same age who obviously had more time for their own personal development and for activities they enjoyed.

My own cousin and her husband had three sons. Two of the boys contracted muscular dystrophy when they were children. One of them recently died in his middle twenties. My family and I have visited these relatives during the past few summers.

We were aware that their family lifestyle was largely determined by the illness of the two boys. Even the architecture of the house showed the effects: there was an internal elevator designed to accommodate wheel chairs and to provide access to all three floors, including the basement. They also have a van equipped with a lifting device which enabled them to take trips and to enjoy their vacation home on a lake in central Minnesota.

Our aunt, a widow who lives near them, has been gracious enough to sit for the parents on many occasions, freeing them to get away and on those occasions at least to feel not quite so circumscribed. Although I have never heard my cousin and her husband complain about the demands on their time, energy, and financial resources, I know they feel the loss of freedom that the parents of handicapped children commonly experience.

The Caring Congregation

Pastoral care through the congregation may be able to give the parents of handicapped children a kind of relief available from no other source: pastors and service groups may be able to arrange for the volunteering of time or the giving of money for babysitting service. Since ideally this is not just a one-time thing, such pastoral care should focus on organization for continual service to families who have handicapped children. As long as such a service is needed, a caring church will provide it.

Emotional support from the members of the congregation is usually needed and often forthcoming. Often overlooked but equally needed and as greatly appreciated by parents of handicapped children is material support. The financial burden on families of the handicapped is usually very great and existing aid and financial support systems cannot begin to provide what is really needed.

The experience of my minister-friend may be rare but it suggests a model worth considering: "The roles were reversed in our case," Molly's father told me. "The congregation has given us pastoral care. The congregation we serve has been especially thoughtful and gracious to us. They have given us money for babysitting and for help in cleaning in our home, often preparing meals when we were having guests. Also," he continued, "they have given us time and money for trips so we could get away for a while. They have been extremely generous to us and have shown us what pastoral care from a congregation to the minister's family can really be like. We are very fortunate to be part of such a congregation."*

What the Congregation Can Do

There are ways in which a congregation can minister to parents of handicapped children. A few of them are suggested here: (1) Enlist volunteers for babysitting or for contributing money for the purpose of hiring the babysitter in order to free the parents for fun and/or activities outside the family. (2) Enlist volunteers for help in house cleaning, cooking, or other needed services, or give money for purchasing such domestic services from organizations in the community. (3) Help the parents to take trips by contributing money to their transportation or recreation expenses, and see that they get help from volunteers or paid persons to care for things at home while they are gone. Sometimes parents may wish to take their handicapped children along, but more often the purpose of such trips is to grant the parents respite from the continual burden they carry and give them a period of time they can call their own. Such times of separation are for the children's sake as well.

Special mention needs to be made of the matter of public pastoral and congregational recognition of parents of disabled children. Some parents find themselves caring for handicapped children who are born into their family. Others come upon the task through adoption or foster-home placement. Handicapped children are rarely considered when parents are looking for a child to adopt. Not all members of congregations are able to open their homes to handicapped children, of course, but some are. Those who can and will are doing a great service to the community, one that should not go unacknowledged in the caring congregation.

Pastors who publicly recognize the natural parents of handicapped children and the parents who adopt handicapped children will make the congregation aware of the tremendous responsibility and care borne by such parents. Whatever form the recognition takes, it should be a way of honoring the parents, not of setting them apart as objects of pity.

In a small town near my city lives a physician and his wife. They have seven children in the family. The unusual thing about this family is that only one of the seven children is the natural child of the couple. The other unusual fact is that all six of the adopted children were, when they first came into the family, handicapped in some way.

The parents learned after the birth of their first child that they could not have more children of their own. They also discovered they would have to wait months before they could adopt a normal child, whereas the handicapped children routinely ignored by other hopeful parents were readily available. Deciding that he as a doctor and she as a former nurse could be a unique team to provide the needed care for handicapped children, they purposely began to adopt such children until they had six in addition to their one.

One of the adopted children had a stomach disability which he has since outgrown; standing six feet five inches tall and weighing 230 pounds, he is now a member of the football team of one of the local colleges, feared by opposing linemen. Two of the children have had heart defects corrected through surgery, and now live active lives. A daughter has had three open heart surgeries, the last more than two years ago. A son has had corrective heart surgery and now plays baseball, basketball, and football for his high school.

All of the children have apparently overcome their defects and are living normal lives. They had the enviable good fortune to be chosen by a dedicated couple who began immediately to take all steps necessary to help the children overcome their various handicaps.

Some may say, "Well, a doctor usually has the financial resources and the basic skills to undertake a project like that." That is probably true. Nevertheless, even though the physician and his wife foresaw possibilities of healing, the venture was still a calculated risk: the efforts to facilitate healing imparted heavy responsibility with no assurance whatever that everything would come out as well as it has. Bold action of that sort requires courage and dedication beyond the ordinary because handicapped children present unusual problems in the way of care. It takes a rare spirit to rear a whole family of them.

Such devotion is often characteristic of natural parents as well. They too should be honored by the pastor and the congregation.

All parents of handicapped children deserve positive "strokes," words of commendation, grateful recognition, for the mission they undertake.

There are numerous other ways in which congregations can extend pastoral care to the parents and families of handicapped children. The options are limited only by the imagination of the people involved.

A congregation can be alert to the physical needs of handicapped children. For their comfort and mobility church architecture can be changed or rooms remodeled to accommodate wheel chairs and other necessary medical devices. Since one of the desired goals in ministry with the handicapped is to aid disabled persons to be as independent as they can be, providing enabing structures for their existence is an important aspect of the congregation's pastoral care.

Family Counseling

Counseling is important to handicapped people. The mother of a cerebral-palsied youth said to me recently, "My son had the best medical care we could give him. He had physical therapy, occupational therapy, and other professional services, but no counseling. I'm sorry about that. We just know he could have benefitted from counseling. He had no opportunity to talk with skilled persons. We feel he is suffering from that lack now."

Counseling is equally important to the families of handicapped children. Without exception among the homes of handicapped children I have visited, family members have said that the family counseling sessions were among the most valuable of the many services extended to them by the various agencies. Though they were in no way discounting other tremendously valuable services, most maintained that for the purpose of getting oriented to the handicapped child's illness or disablement and learning what attitudes and behaviors are most helpful to the child family counseling is highly valued and greatly appreciated. Such family counseling for families of handicapped children normally includes all members of the family from about four years of age on.

In group sessions members of the family are enabled to bring out their own feelings about the handicapped child and about their family relationships. They gain insight into their patterns

ing Relationships

much-heralded high school athlete of our city was
ed recently in an automobile accident. An excit-
ayer, he had thrilled sports fans of the whole city
dible performances. "His running and passing is
behold," a sportswriter once said of him. As
nd team leader—and also a top scholar—he was
f the field as on.
lyzed from the waist down, he was thrust into a
irtual isolation. Whereas doting peers and friends
m the center of adulation, suddenly, almost over-
ere all gone. He was left with the support of only
ate family, who were themselves having trouble
e reality of his handicap.
of human relationships can have a devastating effect
orale of anyone, especially a popular athlete who must
etely revise his image of himself. For months after
the consequences of his injury, the young man did not
e. During that time, however, his girlfriend stood
him. He steadily maintained that he did not want to
ain, but she quietly and patiently refused to abandon
ntually her acceptance triumphed and he began to
acceptance as well as his handicap. Today he is a
ce of inspiration to other young athletes of the city.

Significant Relationships

nships are significant to recovery and to the ongoing
tion which was described earlier in this book. The
vare of the power of relationships will enable handi
ersons to marshal whatever resources they have to fos

of interaction and ways of becoming more mutually supportive.

Parents often resent their handicapped children and tend to feel guilty for doing so. Most siblings are also deeply affected by the feelings and behaviors of the handicapped child. In the case of Molly's family the siblings had to learn what they could and could not expect and do in relation to their afflicted sister. Such knowledge involves learning what behaviors may be hurtful or damaging to the handicapped child. Thus siblings too must learn the meaning of the handicap. The disabled child must learn to know and to control personal behaviors that could be damaging to self or others. Thus siblings, indeed whole families learn together how they can better cope with and support each other.

Pastors can lead such family counseling sessions themselves or simply set them up in the congregation and arrange for others to lead. They can also refer people to places where there is trained leadership and counseling readily available. Pastors can contact organizations operated specifically by and for persons with particular handicaps. At the back of this book I have listed some of the more prominent national organizations whose programs may prove helpful. Further information is often available through the local organization headquarters which are listed in the telephone directory.

Today training is increasingly available for pastors and lay persons interested in counseling with members of families of handicapped persons. The continuing-education publications of many denominations and judicatories list the most recent opportunities for such training; they catalog the special offerings of forthcoming workshops, institutes, seminars, and courses of seminaries, universities, colleges, and other institutions of higher learning.

Residential Placement

The issue of residential placement is a touchy one for most parents of a disabled child. Should they, *can* they "put their child away in an institution"? They recognize the value of having trained staff persons work individually with the child to facilitate growth in knowledge, skills, and relationships. But a sense of guilt attaches to what may resemble child abandonment.

Molly's father put it this way: "The issue of putting Molly in a residential center for handicapped children certainly raised guilt feelings within us which we have continually discussed with each other. It's a case of 'guilty if you do and guilty if you don't.' We feel that as parents we provide a unique love and care that nobody else can give her. Yet we also think about her long-range needs for independence and self-care. Actually, we do not want to deny her either of those, and that is the source of our inner conflict on the matter."

Residential placement has much to commend it: (1) The child may learn to cope with the existential situation and gain some independence from the parents. (2) Residential staff persons may confront the child in ways the parents could not; such trained confrontation and loving support is likely to call out feelings and behaviors conductive to independence and self-responsibility. (3) Peer cooperation and support in the institution tends to encourage the handicapped child toward self-imposition of the requirement for responsible behavior whereas at home overprotectiveness by members of the family may all but preclude the challenge to growth in self-reliance.

Any discussion of residential placement must of course at least mention a couple of the negative factors, which in some cases prove to be of overriding significance:

(1) The available center may be too far away for meaningful family contact on a continuing basis. Centers that can provide the highly trained personnel for working with handicapped children simply do not exist in large numbers. Where I live, people have to think in terms of two centers, both located out of state, that must serve the populations of at least three or four whole states. We need more residential placement homes that are optimally equipped and staffed to do an efficient job in local communities.

(2) The cost of residential care in the homes that do exist and offer the needed facilities and services may be prohibitive for most families. While most parents of handicapped children do not want to make the cost of care and treatment the determining factor, they are faced with the reality of distributing their income rather widely in order to maintain themselves and contribute to the growth of their other children. Most parents of handicapped children will sacrifice greatly to give those children education,

training, and develo
be reasonable in ma

Congregations cou
scholarships or in oth
care and special train
penses can be one of
can do in ministry to
handicapped child in a

The

"What will happen to
minister friend asked plai
happens to her when we
we do now?"

These are agonizing q
children. It is the consider
to look strongly at residen
capped child, despite their
the child.

Pastors can help parents t
spects. They can lead the c
parents about caring for the c
child's care will be paid for.
covenant with each other ab
guaranteeing the long-range sec

We have considered various
gregations can be aware of and
people. The key to effective pa
establishment of meaningful per
trician has spoken eloquently of
on the treatment of autistic childre

Some medications have also prov
the child's awareness and attention
ing to control behavior in themselv
bad; they are not a substitute for
methods teaching, firm limits and dir
and parent-parent, and parent-doctor
ful, trustful relationship.*

Positive and powerful human relation
of handicapped people and give hope

7. Promo

A bright and
critically injur
ing football p
with his incre
something to
quarterback
as popular of

Now para
situation of
had made h
night, they
his immedi
accepting th

The loss
upon the m
now compl
he learned
want to li
loyally by
see her ag
him. Ev
accept he
great sou

Relati
rehabilita
pastor a
capped

ter healing relationships. The pastor's own caring relationship and that of others can be such a resource—of inestimable value to the handicapped person.

There are three types of relationships which serve as primary resources. They shape and strengthen the life of any person, but especially of the disabled person.

The first is an intimate, risky relationship with one's own inner life. In our society we are taught not to trust feelings and behavior which emerge from our inner life. We are told they are too subjective and undependable. However, data springing from our inner life are actually sources of inspiration and creativity, and this needs to be acknowledged.

The second is an intimate, vulnerable relationship with one other person who is trusted implicitly. This is called a love relationship. I give to the one I love a special power, the power to hurt me. The risk is worth taking because the relationship offers fulfillment to those involved in it.

Finally, developing the art of relating to others is of extreme importance. The handicapped person, rather than assuming that other people are turned off by his or her disablement or regard him or her as an alien object to be pitied, can initiate friendly transactions even with strangers and thereby find out how those people actually feel. This involves honest and open self-disclosure in which the handicapped person reveals himself or herself to the other person in an accepting way, thus helping each to feel comfortable and appropriately concerned about one another.

The Flowing Fountain of the Inner Life

The first relationship resource for the handicapped person is thus that of one's own inner self. To touch the great mystery of one's own internal being is to tap a resource of magnitude and promise. Although the act of plumbing one's own depths and thereby overcoming alienation from one's self seems extremely difficult and rare, it is of tremendous consequence to the handicapped person.

In *The Power at the Bottom of the Well* Muriel James and Louis Savary speak of the flow of energy from what they call the

"Inner Core."* Something like this is surely at work among those disabled persons who despite their affliction have the will to live. As the rehabilitation psychologists insisted, such persons depend upon that flow of energy to achieve success in their rehabilitation efforts.

"Do you know that God's Spirit dwells within you?" the Apostle Paul says in his First Letter to the Corinthians (3:16). People reared in a highly technical and rational culture like ours find it difficult to get in touch with that "Inner Core." Often they do not trust the data which come from that source.

James and Savary have called this resource the "Power at the Bottom of the Well." Using 1 Corinthians 3:16 as a kind of text, they assert that energy, vitality, drive, and strength are obtained from this "Inner Core."†

I would change the metaphor somewhat. In order to emphasize the dynamic character of the phenomenon, I call it the "flowing fountain of the inner life."

Carl G. Jung has explained why getting in touch with what he called the "collective unconscious" is so hard for people in Western society. Enamored by technology and the rationalism which kindles it, people have been taught not to trust data which flow from their own inner life. They are thus cut off from a rich source of imagination and creativity. Myths by which people must live, says Jung, are held suspect, and people repress their fantasies. The net result is alienation from the self, which becomes agonizingly critical when a person becomes disabled and isolated from others.‡

Jung says that we tend to develop rituals to protect ourselves from the tremendous threat of that great reservoir of energy and creativity, our collective unconscious. The collective unconscious is that which relates us to earliest primitive man and is primordial within us. Only when we can assimilate what comes from our collective unconscious can we also "individuate," i.e., become unique, competent, energy-directed individuals.§

Jung maintains that dreams are the reliable sources of data for that process.‖ However, I believe that profound dialogue with other people can also stimulate individual excursions into one's own depths, where untold power is available to the person.

of interaction and ways of becoming more mutually supportive. Parents often resent their handicapped children and tend to feel guilty for doing so. Most siblings are also deeply affected by the feelings and behaviors of the handicapped child. In the case of Molly's family the siblings had to learn what they could and could not expect and do in relation to their afflicted sister. Such knowledge involves learning what behaviors may be hurtful or damaging to the handicapped child. Thus siblings too must learn the meaning of the handicap. The disabled child must learn to know and to control personal behaviors that could be damaging to self or others. Thus siblings, indeed whole families learn together how they can better cope with and support each other.

Pastors can lead such family counseling sessions themselves or simply set them up in the congregation and arrange for others to lead. They can also refer people to places where there is trained leadership and counseling readily available. Pastors can contact organizations operated specifically by and for persons with particular handicaps. At the back of this book I have listed some of the more prominent national organizations whose programs may prove helpful. Further information is often available through the local organization headquarters which are listed in the telephone directory.

Today training is increasingly available for pastors and lay persons interested in counseling with members of families of handicapped persons. The continuing-education publications of many denominations and judicatories list the most recent opportunities for such training; they catalog the special offerings of forthcoming workshops, institutes, seminars, and courses of seminaries, universities, colleges, and other institutions of higher learning.

Residential Placement

The issue of residential placement is a touchy one for most parents of a disabled child. Should they, *can* they "put their child away in an institution"? They recognize the value of having trained staff persons work individually with the child to facilitate growth in knowledge, skills, and relationships. But a sense of guilt attaches to what may resemble child abandonment.

Molly's father put it this way: "The issue of putting Molly in a residential center for handicapped children certainly raised guilt feelings within us which we have continually discussed with each other. It's a case of 'guilty if you do and guilty if you don't.' We feel that as parents we provide a unique love and care that nobody else can give her. Yet we also think about her long-range needs for independence and self-care. Actually, we do not want to deny her either of those, and that is the source of our inner conflict on the matter."

Residential placement has much to commend it: (1) The child may learn to cope with the existential situation and gain some independence from the parents. (2) Residential staff persons may confront the child in ways the parents could not; such trained confrontation and loving support is likely to call out feelings and behaviors conductive to independence and self-responsibility. (3) Peer cooperation and support in the institution tends to encourage the handicapped child toward self-imposition of the requirement for responsible behavior whereas at home overprotectiveness by members of the family may all but preclude the challenge to growth in self-reliance.

Any discussion of residential placement must of course at least mention a couple of the negative factors, which in some cases prove to be of overriding significance:

(1) The available center may be too far away for meaningful family contact on a continuing basis. Centers that can provide the highly trained personnel for working with handicapped children simply do not exist in large numbers. Where I live, people have to think in terms of two centers, both located out of state, that must serve the populations of at least three or four whole states. We need more residential placement homes that are optimally equipped and staffed to do an efficient job in local communities.

(2) The cost of residential care in the homes that do exist and offer the needed facilities and services may be prohibitive for most families. While most parents of handicapped children do not want to make the cost of care and treatment the determining factor, they are faced with the reality of distributing their income rather widely in order to maintain themselves and contribute to the growth of their other children. Most parents of handicapped children will sacrifice greatly to give those children education,

training, and developmental opportunities, but they do have to be reasonable in making commitments that cost money.

Congregations could help in many instances by providing scholarships or in other ways contributing to the costs of home care and special training. Sharing some of the staggering expenses can be one of the most significant things a congregation can do in ministry to families who are struggling to place their handicapped child in a residential placement center.

The Long-Range Future

"What will happen to Molly if something happens to us?" my minister friend asked plaintively. "Or, what is more likely, what happens to her when we are no longer able to give her the care we do now?"

These are agonizing questions for parents of handicapped children. It is the consideration of such issues that leads parents to look strongly at residential placement centers for a handicapped child, despite their emotional resistance to "giving up" the child.

Pastors can help parents to think through the long-range prospects. They can lead the congregation in negotiating with the parents about caring for the child or in assuring parents that the child's care will be paid for. Congregation and parents may covenant with each other about sharing the responsibility of guaranteeing the long-range security of the child.

We have considered various ways in which pastors and congregations can be aware of and support families of handicapped people. The key to effective pastoral care lies, of course, in the establishment of meaningful personal relationships. A pediatrician has spoken eloquently of such relationships as they bear on the treatment of autistic children:

> Some medications have also proved helpful in helping increase the child's awareness and attention span. These drugs do nothing to control behavior in themselves or make a child good or bad; they are not a substitute for loving acceptance, special methods teaching, firm limits and direction, one-on-one attention, and parent-parent, and parent-doctor communications in a truthful, trustful relationship.*

Positive and powerful human relationships can enhance the lives of handicapped people and give hope to all concerned.

7. Promoting Relationships

A bright and much-heralded high school athlete of our city was critically injured recently in an automobile accident. An exciting football player, he had thrilled sports fans of the whole city with his incredible performances. "His running and passing is something to behold," a sportswriter once said of him. As quarterback and team leader—and also a top scholar—he was as popular off the field as on.

Now paralyzed from the waist down, he was thrust into a situation of virtual isolation. Whereas doting peers and friends had made him the center of adulation, suddenly, almost overnight, they were all gone. He was left with the support of only his immediate family, who were themselves having trouble accepting the reality of his handicap.

The loss of human relationships can have a devastating effect upon the morale of anyone, especially a popular athlete who must now completely revise his image of himself. For months after he learned the consequences of his injury, the young man did not want to live. During that time, however, his girlfriend stood loyally by him. He steadily maintained that he did not want to see her again, but she quietly and patiently refused to abandon him. Eventually her acceptance triumphed and he began to accept her acceptance as well as his handicap. Today he is a great source of inspiration to other young athletes of the city.

Significant Relationships

Relationships are significant to recovery and to the ongoing rehabilitation which was described earlier in this book. The pastor aware of the power of relationships will enable handicapped persons to marshal whatever resources they have to foster healing relationships. The pastor's own caring relationship and that of others can be such a resource—of inestimable value to the handicapped person.

There are three types of relationships which serve as primary resources. They shape and strengthen the life of any person, but especially of the disabled person.

The first is an intimate, risky relationship with one's own inner life. In our society we are taught not to trust feelings and behavior which emerge from our inner life. We are told they are too subjective and undependable. However, data springing from our inner life are actually sources of inspiration and creativity, and this needs to be acknowledged.

The second is an intimate, vulnerable relationship with one other person who is trusted implicitly. This is called a love relationship. I give to the one I love a special power, the power to hurt me. The risk is worth taking because the relationship offers fulfillment to those involved in it.

Finally, developing the art of relating to others is of extreme importance. The handicapped person, rather than assuming that other people are turned off by his or her disablement or regard him or her as an alien object to be pitied, can initiate friendly transactions even with strangers and thereby find out how those people actually feel. This involves honest and open self-disclosure in which the handicapped person reveals himself or herself to the other person in an accepting way, thus helping each to feel comfortable and appropriately concerned about one another.

The Flowing Fountain of the Inner Life

The first relationship resource for the handicapped person is thus that of one's own inner self. To touch the great mystery of one's own internal being is to tap a resource of magnitude and promise. Although the act of plumbing one's own depths and thereby overcoming alienation from one's self seems extremely difficult and rare, it is of tremendous consequence to the handicapped person.

In *The Power at the Bottom of the Well* Muriel James and Louis Savary speak of the flow of energy from what they call the

"Inner Core."* Something like this is surely at work among those disabled persons who despite their affliction have the will to live. As the rehabilitation psychologists insisted, such persons depend upon that flow of energy to achieve success in their rehabilitation efforts.

"Do you know that God's Spirit dwells within you?" the Apostle Paul says in his First Letter to the Corinthians (3:16). People reared in a highly technical and rational culture like ours find it difficult to get in touch with that "Inner Core." Often they do not trust the data which come from that source.

James and Savary have called this resource the "Power at the Bottom of the Well." Using 1 Corinthians 3:16 as a kind of text, they assert that energy, vitality, drive, and strength are obtained from this "Inner Core."†

I would change the metaphor somewhat. In order to emphasize the dynamic character of the phenomenon, I call it the "flowing fountain of the inner life."

Carl G. Jung has explained why getting in touch with what he called the "collective unconscious" is so hard for people in Western society. Enamored by technology and the rationalism which kindles it, people have been taught not to trust data which flow from their own inner life. They are thus cut off from a rich source of imagination and creativity. Myths by which people must live, says Jung, are held suspect, and people repress their fantasies. The net result is alienation from the self, which becomes agonizingly critical when a person becomes disabled and isolated from others.‡

Jung says that we tend to develop rituals to protect ourselves from the tremendous threat of that great reservoir of energy and creativity, our collective unconscious. The collective unconscious is that which relates us to earliest primitive man and is primordial within us. Only when we can assimilate what comes from our collective unconscious can we also "individuate," i.e., become unique, competent, energy-directed individuals.§

Jung maintains that dreams are the reliable sources of data for that process.‖ However, I believe that profound dialogue with other people can also stimulate individual excursions into one's own depths, where untold power is available to the person.

Disciplined meditation is a method of getting in touch with the flowing fountain of the inner life. In the Eastern world meditation has long been emphasized. We of the Western world have tended not to trust it. Recently, however, the practice of the contemplative life has been more evident in our country. Jung had seen the need for such corrective to our preoccupation with objectivity.*

The pastor's acceptance and reinforcement of expressions from the inner life of handicapped persons is a significant way of affirming the value of such persons to the community in which they live. Their value is in their total being. That kind of affirmation is tremendously reassuring to persons living in a society which places such a high premium on a person's productivity.

Intimate Vulnerable Relationship
with Another Person

For the paraplegic, the terminal cancer patient, the stroke victim, the kidney patient, and other disabled persons the possibility of an intimate, vulnerable relationship with another person often seems, after disablement, utterly remote. Those who have already had an intimate relationship may or may not be fortunate enough to have the continuing loyalty and commitment of a loving partner.

I know dialysis patients better than other disabled persons. I am aware that many marriages of dialysis patients have not survived the earliest experiences of the spouse's illness. Others do not make it through the training period. Still others may go along for a while, then collapse of weariness with the whole routine. Often personal attitudes on the part of the kidney patient toward his or her own illness trigger feelings in the spouse that she or he cannot tolerate the situation any further.

A dialysis technician chided a nurse who had been asked for a date by a kidney patient: "OK, but don't fall in love with a dialysis patient. Surely you don't want to take on that burden!" Her only comment was: "I work here too remember; I know what it's like. "Then with a flip of her head and a teasing tone of voice she added, "And anyway, I'll fall in love with whomever I want to!"

Many spouses, as in my own case, are deeply committed to "running their mates on the machine." In fact the wife of one of my dialysis friends felt so useless after his successful kidney transplant that she had to work through difficult feelings about that lost role.

Nevertheless many disabled persons who have not had an intimate relationship prior to the disabling accident or illness despair of finding someone who will care that much for them. Even when love does happen some handicapped persons tend to distrust it, believing they are objects of pity or of some other nonauthentic motive.

Ernest Coffin, the late editor of *DAY* (Dialysis and You) magazine for dialysis and kidney transplant patients, had kidney disease from childhood until young manhood, when he was chosen from about two hundred candidates to be placed on a kidney machine. He wrote about his relationship with his nurse:

> I found myself, at the suggestion of a nurse-friend, sitting face to face with a psychologist who was to help me radically change my whole life. After several moments of silence she said, "Dialysis is pretty awful, isn't it?" I tried to deny it, but even as I did I realized I had used dialysis as a scapegoat for all my failures. Inside I disliked myself and so rejected the love of family and friends before they would have the chance to reject me. Blaming dialysis for all my troubles, I became lonely and isolated. After all, who would want a dialysis patient for a friend, or a lover, or a husband?
>
> All of these feelings which I had never before been able to organize and understand, she led me gently through. . . . The turning point came at the end of the first painful session. As I was about to leave, my mind completely boggled with what I had learned about myself, she said simply, "Ernie, I really like you." I walked out of the office with tears streaming down my face.
>
> For so long I feared to show love, to care, or to be a friend and share any of my real feelings. I was learning to accept those feelings and to trust another human being. . . .
>
> At about the same time I met, in Silva Mind Control classes, a beautiful woman who was a nurse and who cared deeply for other people. Because of her career, nothing about dialysis offended her. We grew to have a strong friendship and I began programming that she would come to love me. I was approved for home dialysis and she agreed to be my partner. . . .
>
> By this time I was deeply in love with her so that when she

suggested that we bring the machine to her condominium so that she could avoid that two-hour travel time and get more rest, I was euphoric. . . .
We did everything as a team, we played, we worked, we socialized, and often we were angry at the same things. As I went through the ups and downs of coil ruptures [the kidney coil which cleans the blood], low hematocrits [red blood cell count], and depressions with dialysis and the magazine, she kept reaching out to me and loving me and working out our problems. She made me feel like a whole person. Suddenly I had everything I had always wanted—love, a wife, a son, and a caring community of friends who supported us as we dealt with dialysis. We've worked at our relationship, discussing every hurt, honestly expressing anger, and always expecting the very best from each other, so that we have goals to achieve. . . . in short, through being loved and living I've found a way to find real happiness for myself on dialysis*

The intimate, vulnerable relationship often ends with a parting or separation. Indeed, such was the case for Ernest Coffin. A few months after his third kidney transplant he developed a raging fever and died of what was diagnosed as pneumonia. After his death the "beautiful woman" nurse who shared his final years wrote a tribute which was published in *DAY*, the magazine he had founded:

I had to accept early in our relationship that no matter how much I loved him, *I was not responsible in any way for his illness.* . . . I soon learned that for Ernie to be in control of his life and lead as normal a life as possible, he needed a strong woman who was also leading a normal life. We had to continue to grow as individuals each dealing with his or her own problems before we could live together maximally as a couple.
We discovered the example we presented of independent and combined strengths encouraged other single dialysis persons to believe in themselves and *search for someone to share their lives with.*†

She plunged into the work Ernie had started on the magazine in order to prevent herself from being immobilized by the pain and loneliness she was feeling. Their intimate relationship had meant vulnerability for both of them. She was experiencing the pain of the inevitable separation when it came. Yet she was grateful for the years she had spent with him. However vulnerable it made them, their love had been fulfilling for both. The message in Ernest Coffin's story is clear. The intimate, vulnerable relationship, while risky, is tremendously satisfying to handicapped persons and to those who love them.

Relating to Others

People who can establish an intimate, vulnerable relationship, and do so, usually value and accept themselves as well. They learn to say with feeling: "I am me, the most important person in the world." This is not, however, an expression of self-centeredness. On the contrary, what it articulates is an acceptance of one's own self.

Self-acceptance generates acceptance of other people. "Love your neighbor as yourself," Jesus is purported to have said as he enunciated a principle which is obviously central to the gospel. Bernard Meland speaks of the action required to fulfill this principle in terms of developing an "appreciative consciousness."* It is a matter of admiring goodness wherever it is found, in all the people about us.

As a handicapped person who lives on the boundary between life and death I find that I value life so much that I appreciate immensely the people I meet. I see more positive qualities in such people than I have ever seen before. Not that I am looking at people or at the world through rose-colored glasses that obscure my vision of the reality of crippling inertia in people. However, I am less prone to be negatively critical of people's apparent unwillingness to change. I am much more confident now of people's inmost desire to remove all barriers to their own self-actualization. For me the level of trust toward others and hope in others has been lifted. My appreciative consciousness of all people, even strangers, has been raised.

The action of expressing an appreciative consciousness is sometimes referred to, in the language of Transactional Analysis and its founder Eric Berne, as the giving of "strokes."† Strokes can be either positive or negative, verbal or nonverbal. They are acts of stimulating the spinal cord which basically give one a feeling about himself or herself. Positive strokes tend to "stretch" the spinal cord, leaving the person with a feeling of well-being; they contribute to a healthy self-concept. Negative strokes—or the total absence of strokes—causes a "shrinking" of the spinal cord; they give one bad feelings about himself or herself.*

Pastors are always giving strokes, whether positive or negative. The pastor's very presence with another person is a stroke of sorts. What is important for the handicapped person is the pastor's self-revelation. Pastoring persons can do more than simply approve or condemn—they can relate! They can so disclose and share their humanity, their person, their caring concern, that persons come to feel it, even accept and reciprocate it. The relationship with the pastor can be a model of supportive relating. Indeed, herein is the reality of grace. "The reality of God as concrete occurrence is discerned not as abstract Being or Process, but as the primordial and providential goodness within relationships, the efficacy of which adheres in every event of creativity, sensitivity, and negotiability by which relationships are sustained; or when broken, restored; and by which such relationships are made redemptive and healing is a work of judgment and grace."†

This statement of Bernard Meland articulates theologically a ground for the pastor's self-revelation as caring person. The pastor may be the key not just to one such open and supportive relationship but to others as well. The development or restoration of such relationships is of critical importance to the disabled person: psychologically they can mean the difference between life and death. An important pastoral tool among the vehicles for growth—important also for psychological fulfillment in terms of the relationships it provides—is the small group.

8. Sustaining Support Systems

A man with powerfully built shoulders deftly whisked his wheel chair into position at the side of the church aisle. He had been transported to the church in a van especially built for him. "I have always felt that I belong here," he said to me with a smile. "These people have accepted me since poliomyelitis struck me back in the 1950s. What disappointed me at that time was that the minister seemed to be afraid to visit me. He apparently feared he might carry the disease to his young family. I don't know. Maybe he was afraid of getting polio himself. He didn't say. Anyway, I kept wanting to talk to him, but he avoided seeing me. The congregation itself was more accepting and supportive."

Without bitterness this man, whom I shall call Michael, went on to express in detail his feelings of abandonment by the pastor and acceptance by the congregation. He said he was grateful to the worshiping community for the tremendous support he had received when he most needed it. It was reassuring, Michael acknowledged, to feel he had a group who appreciated him, who valued and accepted him, indeed, who loved him.

Everyone needs such experience of a supportive community, especially handicapped people. The handicapped feel that they are among the alienated of our society. They need, at a feeling level, the experience of alienation overcome. Pastoral support can be the key to such experience.

Sustaining the Disabled

As in case of death and bereavement, the mode of pastoral care most appropriate to the person who has experienced loss is supportive pastoral care. Insight-oriented therapies are not indicated in such cases, but supportive counseling, supplemented by behavior modification, aids and abets the natural healing process. Supportive care seeks to impart strength through standing by. To stand by the person means to be available, present to that person, not with ready advice or pat answers, but with concern, care, and empathy, however mute, in face of the grief and loss.

Seward Hiltner uses the word *sustaining* to indicate what is meant here:

> But *sustaining* is meant that aspect of the shepherding perspective that emphasizes standing by! Unlike healing, in which the total situation is capable of change, sustaining relates to situations that as total situations cannot be changed or at least cannot be changed at this time. . . . Sustaining is the ministry of support and encouragement through standing by when what had been a whole has been broken, or impaired, and is incapable of total situational restoration, at least now *

In his discussion of the difference between sustaining and the popular understanding of comfort Hiltner says: "Comfort is not consolation but silent companionship."†

Webster's Dictionary defines *sustain* as: "to keep from sinking or falling, especially by bearing up from below—to keep from sinking into despondency or discouragement."‡ Literally the Latin root word *sustineo* means "to hold up or bear up."

In the act of silent companionship the pastoring person gives sufficient strength to the people in crisis for them to do their grief work. Sustaining in the sense intended here means standing *by*, not standing in *for*: the pastor does not take away from the disabled person's own responsibility for working through the grief. A scriptural passage, although spoken in a different context, puts the matter well: "Bear one another's burdens, and so fulfill the law of Christ. . . . But let each one test his own work. . . . For each man will have to bear his own load" (Gal. 6:2–5). Paul was originally discussing attitudes toward someone who had trespassed; he was concerned that such a person be reprehended gently and restored to fellowship. I have used his words in the broader sense of taking responsibility yet not "taking over" for a person in any crisis.

So regarded, sustaining is an enabling task. As I have said

throughout, the initial shock of any devastating illness or accident tends to leave the person shattered and without support. Healing within the person will go on, but the affected person needs someone to lean on. A sustaining other can help hold the person together—keep the person from falling apart—during the shock phase of the disablement.

The Support System

Whereas the personal presence of the pastor can be significantly sustaining, particularly in the early stages, ongoing pastoral care often calls for the creation of a support system. Something like a small group has existed in the church since its inception. Small groups in the modern congregation give strength, support, and encouragement to their members. They can enhance a disabled person's will to live. I have had several handicapped persons in my groups, and I have been thrilled to see how, with the unflagging support of the group, each of them has developed a positive self-concept.

There are various structures and approaches that can serve the support group. The approach may be that of Gestalt therapy, with emphasis upon getting feelings and behavior together in the here-and-now.* It may be that of Transactional Analysis, with contract-setting so that the group members can act on what they want to change about themselves or their relationships with other people.† It may be that of an encounter group, wherein people are free to express their feelings toward each other and behave toward each other within such limits as they have set for themselves.‡ Or it may involve a combination of two or more of these modes. Indeed, other structures for group life may also be developed. Any or all of these styles for group meetings can prove beneficial for handicapped persons. Whatever the mode of group life, as long as the experience is one in which the dignity and potentiality of each person involved is the central focus, the person usually emerges at some point with a positively enhanced self-image.

It was only after struggling with my own illness in comparative isolation for almost a year that I discovered the camaraderie of small groups of kidney patients. Also at about that time I became aware of the enjoyment of participating with other patients in meetings of the Indiana Kidney Foundation. The fellowship with similarly afflicted persons has been, in my experience, tremendously supportive.

On occasion, when my secretary has driven me to the hospital for a clinic visit, she has waited for me in the reception area, an intimate setting in which patients sit in a small rectangle of chairs and converse easily with each other. Once as we were leaving the clinic following my regular checkup she remarked about the experience: "I felt rather strange there. It was almost like being in a different world. I felt uneasy, as if I were looking in on something very private and I didn't belong. The patients seemed so tuned in to each other that they were hardly aware of anyone around them."

I acknowledged the reality of her observation. I also explained to her how significant this group is for me. It constitutes a part of my support system.

It is important for pastors to recognize that an operative support system is a kind of church-in-miniature. A common background of experience and a similar future unite people into a community which has its own language and behavior patterns, its own focal concerns and solidifying empathy.

A support group of disabled persons may be so cohesive as to be functionally exclusive. For the most part, of course, spouses of patients also participate readily in that inner circle because they are usually as involved in the treatment process as the patients themselves. In my experience, however, friends and neighbors too begin to enter the magic circle as they learn how the kidney machine functions and how they too can become effectively supportive. One of my neighbors, for example, the wife of a skilled laborer now retired, regularly visits my home when I am on the machine (and often when I am not). Offering encouragement and help which is greatly appreciated, she thoughtfully does little chores around the house, yet honors our privacy as well, especially when aspects of the process require intense concentration. Thus there can be a considerable circle of friends, relatives, and groups included in any person's support system. The pastor may wish to be among them.

Supportive Counseling

Sometimes the pastor's foremost contribution may come at the point of individual counseling. According to psychiatrist Franz Alexander, supportive counseling involves five basic procedures*:

(1) Gratifying dependency needs. One of the serious problems of handicapped persons is that of dependency on others. The more independent they can be, the better they feel about themselves. Nonetheless, knowing that in specific ways, perhaps for the rest of their life, they will require help from other people, they need to learn how to adjust to this reality. Counseling can be extremely helpful in dealing with this dependence/independence tension.

(2) Permitting emotional catharsis. I find it purifying to let out my feelings about my dialysis. I try to get negative feelings out of my system. When such feelings are expressed they are less likely to get me bogged down in despair. Maurice Ireland, my paraplegic friend, witnesses to the same reality: as he was able to express and vent his feelings about his condition, he could better accept the reality of his handicap. Counseling offers a unique opportunity for such expression.

(3) Objectively reviewing the stress situation. Occasionally I had a difficult time believing it was actually I who was going through the process of dialysis. Having all my life had a proud and strong self-image, it seemed to me at times as if I were having a weird nightmare from which I would probably one day awake. Recently handicapped persons experience that phenomenon. However, when we have the opportunity to talk about the anxiety we feel, we accept better the reality of the entire situation; stress is diminished and we are once again free to make intelligent decisions. Counseling can enhance this sense of reality and of freedom.

(4) Aiding the ego's defenses. Handicapped persons may figure that they were themselves responsible, to a greater or lesser degree, for what actually happened. They may also repress that knowledge as being too terribly painful to bear. Supportive counseling can aid the handicapped in maintaining what they need as an ego defense against whatever shame, guilt, or embar-

rassment they feel. Eventually they may be able to face the truth about their responsibility and, accepting the reality, rid themselves of such ego defenses. Support groups are particularly valuable at this point.

(5) Changing the life situation. Inevitably the person will need to change his or her lifestyle to take into account the particular handicap. The pastor can aid this process by consulting with the person about the possibilities for change that may exist in one or more aspects of the environment.

Howard Clinebell has found these several procedures of supportive counseling relevant also in pastoral counseling.* He has even added two more to those suggested by Franz Alexander:

(6) Engaging in action therapy. In the past, many therapies seemed to stop when the person gained insight into his or her problems and/or self. What apparently was lacking in an exclusive focus on insight therapy was any strong confrontation of the patient by the therapist relative to what would now be *done* about the situation. In contemporary therapies emphasis is increasingly being given to the matter of taking appropriate action. In this connection the small group gives a powerful sanction to responsible action. It holds a person accountable. If a person makes a commitment to specific action, the chances are that that person will indeed act on that commitment rather than face the group again and confess inaction.

(7) Using religious resources. As Clinebell points out, the pastor has certain other tools and procedures which are distinctive: "Prayer, scripture, devotional literature, communion, etc. constitute valuable supportive resources which are unique to pastoral counseling."† Such resources are best used within the framework of an ongoing pastoral relationship.

The Healing Community

Harold H. Wilke, a minister of the United Church of Christ and himself a disabled person since birth, has given leadership to the organization of groups in local parishes across the country which are designed to help the religious community become more conscious of its supportive role in relation to persons with special needs. Functioning without arms, Mr. Wilke has become highly competent at caring for himself with his feet. His skill is so remarkable that people are hardly aware of his disablement.

His project, entitled "The Healing Community," has been in operation now for several years.* It is a national program constructed for the purpose of consciousness-raising in the religious community with respect to potentially alienated persons. Its goal is to help religious groups in giving social acceptance so that the handicapped person can enter the mainstream of national and community life. So far as I know, The Healing Community is the only program in which a concerted effort is made to bring national attention to the church's responsibility to and opportunity with handicapped people.

The organization develops interfaith groups in local communities composed of religious leaders and concerned lay persons. It provides direction through publishing a manual and through meetings, offers consultant services, sets up pilot projects as models, and raises money for the support of the projects. Four of these models aim at responding to the potentially alienated person.

The first is designed especially for Vietnam veterans who are disabled. Its goal goes beyond support to include a focus on the veteran's alienation from a post-Vietnam society.

The second model is being developed to serve a much larger number of persons, those who have been injured in various accidents or stricken by illnesses. This model also envisions support for persons with both related disabilities.

The third model is for persons who have been alienated through drug use. It also serves a number of Vietnam veterans in this connection.

The fourth is an overseas model. It is concerned with an international kind of sharing of community responses to handicapped persons.†

All of these models are implemented in local groups throughout the world. It is these local groups that take responsibility for consciousness-raising in congregations. All the models also make use of audio-visual as well as personal resources. Together they constitute an intensive and comprehensive effort to reconcile handicapped persons with religious communities. The project is extremely valuable and worth developing in every community. As funds and personnel become available the models will probably expand beyond their present sites in New York, Indiana, and California.

Reconciling the Alienated

Larger numbers of persons are routinely injured in industrial, automobile, and other accidents every year. They require the same kind of rehabilitation services as injured soldiers. Millions more have disabilities dating to birth or to early illness and accident in infancy or childhood. Taken together, these persons constitute a significant number of people. And persons who require rehabilitation usually also experience degrees of alienation from others.*

As the household of God, the church has a tremendous challenge and opportunity to work toward the reconciliation of these alienated persons. The pastor's leadership just in consciousness-raising about the problem can be tremendously significant.

Although the Apostle Paul was definitely referring to the enmity between Jews and Gentiles in the second chapter of his Letter to the Ephesians, he could have been speaking to any alienated group. "This was his purpose," he said, referring to Christ's death, "to reconcile the two in a single body to God through the cross *on which he killed the enmity* (v. 16, NEB; italics mine). In fact *all* enmity was killed on the cross. "So he came and proclaimed the good news; peace to you who were afar off, and peace to those who were nearby; for through him we both alike have access to the Father in the one Spirit. Thus you are no longer aliens in a foreign land, but fellow-citizens with God's people, members of God's household" (Ephesians 2: 17–19, NEB).

In an article published by the *Christian Century* entitled "Mainstreaming' the Alienated: The Church Responds to a 'New' Minority," Wilke says the following about the church's ministry to handicapped persons:

> A Lady Bountiful attitude which assumes that the ministry of the church is *to* such unfortunate individuals—rather than *with*

them—misses the whole point of the gospel. . . . Some of the
criteria [for healing communities] . . . are these: (1) The healing
community is supportive of individuals in it; (2) it must cope
with the question of how much it will impose conformity and
whether such imposition is inevitable or necessarily repressive;
(3) it has self-awareness; (4) it can adapt to change and growth;
(5) it is small enough to function effectively; (6) in some cases it
may be involved in institutionalizing in order to reach out in love
and service to those outside the group.*

Most of these points are self-evident and are basic to opening up
the church to a ministry to the disabled.   Item 2 deals with the
question of whether churches are sufficiently flexible.

Some churches by their very architecture do not encourage
handicapped persons to attend.   For example, they may not be
conveniently designed to facilitate the movement of people in
wheelchairs.   In their very structure and appearance they give
the impression that disabled persons are not wanted.   In my own
church, which is on the ground floor, Maurice Ireland attends
regularly.   A paraplegic, he is able to pilot his own wheelchair
into the sanctuary where he is assigned a place in the aisle.

Wilke points out in his article that there are some churches
which minister *only* to handicapped persons.   He cites as examples the Church of the Exceptional, in Macon, Georgia, and
the Victim Missionaries, based in the convent of Our Lady of
Snows, in Belleview, Illinois.†   These are models for church
organizations which serve disabled persons.   They are clearly
supportive.   More integrated churches can additionally help to
overcome the prevailing alienation.

Support and Pastoral Care

Ministers whose churches are not a part of the program I have
just described may wish to organize support groups in their own
churches.   Such groups can offer handicapped persons the much
needed assurance that they are wanted and accepted in the
church.

Support Groups

Pastors who wish to organize support groups may either lead
such groups themselves or find people in the community who will

give leadership to the effort. Pastors may secure special training in various group modes such as Gestalt and Transactional Analysis. Opportunities for such training are readily available in or near most communities. Pastors also need to make supportive statements from the pulpit, expressing sentiments which may help change the attitudes of people toward the disabled.

Congregational groups should include "normal" people as well as handicapped persons, the better to help the latter overcome whatever stigma may be associated with their disability. Members of the congregation who are not in these groups can be tremendously supportive as they get what Wilke calls a deeper "understanding of biblical acceptance of all of God's children."* Church-sponsored groups may help to overcome the isolation and alienation often felt by the disabled. As members of the group they have the opportunity to express thoughts and feelings and to feel the support of other individuals who have experienced similar trauma through illness or injury.

Preaching

Preachers can issue an invitation to all the alienated of the community, including the handicapped and disabled. The biblical grounds for such preaching are manifest.

In several of his parables Jesus is said to have emphasized the ultimate value of every single person. In the context of a parable on humility he stated that one must become as humble as a child "to enter the kingdom of heaven," and he added: "Never despite one of these little ones [referring to the children around him]; I tell you they have their guardian angels in heaven" (Matt. 18:10, NEB).

"So he told them this parable: 'What man of you, having a hundred sheep, if he has lost one of them, does not leave the ninety-nine in the wilderness, and go after the one which is lost, until he finds it? And when he has found it, he lays it on his shoulders, rejoicing' " (Luke 15:3-5). Doesn't this also apply to the one who is injured or ill? Should there not be as much rejoicing over his return as in the case of any other person?

Preaching on such a theme, or on others directed to a similar concern for the reconciliation of "the halt, the lame, and the blind," the minister can help overcome the alienation which the handicapped person feels. Preaching can help to establish the church as the healing community, the household of God that is more bent on including than excluding. In essence that has always been the church's understanding of itself. The church that is diligent in its search for the one lost sheep is fulfilling the biblical-theological understanding of its fundamental ministry with disabled persons.

Ongoing Support

To sustain means to stand by. Standing by in understanding and strength involves: (1) continuing pastoral concern and support, (2) acceptance by the congregation shown by open invitations from members of the congregation to disabled persons to be part of the church, (3) including disabled persons in planning the architecture and programs of the church, and (4) organizing groups which implement the church's function as a healing community.

Notes

Page

xi. *Harold H. Wilke, " 'Mainstreaming' the Alienated: The Church Responds to a 'New' Minority," *Christian Century,* March 23, 1977, p. 272.

1. *I am indebted to John Brantner, Professor of Psychology at the School of Psychiatry, University of Minnesota, for the two stories related here about cracks in the case of the lute and the violins. I am also grateful to him for stimulating my thought about how to conceptualize my own illness. The occasion was a lecture at Christian Theological Seminary, under the auspices of the National Funeral Directors' Association, in which Dr. Brantner was dealing with the theme of Death and Dying.

2. *Virginia Satir, *Peoplemaking* (Palo Alto, California: Science and Behavior Books, Inc. 1972), p. xi. Virginia Satir addresses families, saying she believes the family process concerns self-worth, communication, system, and rules. I am using the term to describe the whole process of encouraging the development of potential in people.

2. †*Webster's New International Dictionary,* 3d ed., s.v. "person." The Latin derivative is *persona,* "actor's mask," or "character in a play."

2. ‡Ibid., s.v. "chastening."

3. *Elisabeth Kübler-Ross, *On Death and Dying* (New York. Macmillan Co., 1969), pp. 38–112.

4. *Webster's New International Dictionary,* 3d ed., s.v. "state."

8. *Harold H. Wilke, *Using Everything You've Got* (The National Easter Seal Society for Crippled Children, 1977).

9. *Carl G. Jung, "Answer to Job," in *The Portable Jung,* ed. Joseph Campbell (New York: Viking Press, 1971), p. 549.

9. †Paul Tillich, *The Courage to Be* (New Haven: Yale University Press, 1952), pp. 9 ff.

9. ‡Ibid., p. 18.

19. *Lois and Arthur Jaffe, "Terminal Candor and the Coda Syn-

drome: A Tandem View of Illness," in *New Meaning of Death,* ed. Herman Feifel (New York: McGraw-Hill Book Co., 1977), p. 210.

20. *My hosts were two psychologists, Richard H. Bost and Edward J. DeVries, and I am indebted to them for the insight that the rehabilitation of handicapped people works best when a strong will to live is present.

24. *Karl Menninger, *Love Against Hate* (New York: Harcourt Brace Jovanovich, 1942), p. 294.

24. †Kahlil Gibran, *The Prophet* (New York: A. A. Knopf, 1923), p. 20.

24. ‡Dwight D. Eisenhower, in *The International Dictionary of Thoughts,* ed. John P. Bradley et al. (Chicago: J. G. Ferguson Co., 1969), p. 318.

24. §William Wordsworth, in ibid., p. 418.

25. *Susan Polis Shutz, *Come into the Mountains, Dear Friend* (Boulder, Colo.: Blue Mountain Arts, Inc., 1972), p. 13.

25. †Harold H. Wilke, *Strengthened with Might* (Philadelphia: Westminster Press, 1952), pp. 75–77. Also see this book for additional suggestions for devotional literature.

27. *Walter B. Cannon, *The Wisdom of the Body* (New York: W. W. Norton & Co., Inc., 1939), p. 20.

27. †Ludwig Von Bertalanffy, *General System Theory* (New York: George Braziller, 1968), p. 39.

28. *Rollo May, *The Meaning of Anxiety* (New York: Ronald Press Co., 1950), p. 191.

29. *Abraham H. Maslow, *Motivation and Personality* (New York: Harper & Row, 1954).

29. †Abraham H. Maslow, *Toward a Psychology of Being* (Princeton: D. Van Nostrand Co., Inc., 1962), p. 43.

30. *Ibid., p. 45.

30. †Ibid.

30. ‡Ibid., p. 47.

31. *World Book Encyclopedia,* s.v. "Demosthenes."

32. *See Kurt Goldstein, *The Organism* (New York: The American Book Co., 1939), p. 50.

32. †Ibid., p. 388.

32. ‡Ibid., p. 434.

35. *Thomas O. Mooney, Theodore M. Cole, and Richard A. Chilgren, *Sexual Options for Paraplegics and Quadraplegics,* with a foreword by Alex Comfort (Boston: Little, Brown, and Co., 1975), p. viii.

37. *Ibid., p. x.
37. †Ibid., (italics by L.G.C.).
37. ‡Ibid., p. ix.
37. §Ibid., p. 1.
37. ‖Ibid.
37. #Ibid.
39. *Ibid., p. 5.
39. †A publication list is available from Theodore M. Cole, Professor, Department of Physical Medicine and Rehabilitation; Director, Physical Disability Program in Human Sexuality, University of Minnesota Medical School. It is entitled *Sexuality and Physical Disability.* I have listed some but not all of the available publications in the Annotated Bibliography at the back of the book. I have listed only the titles which have been published in book form. Articles by this group of associates also appear in various journals, the titles of which may be obtained from the University of Minnesota.
46. *This statement is from a recent interview with Molly's parents. Although I had known them before Molly's birth, I had not previously talked with them specifically about their experiences with her.
51. *Marvin L. Bittinger, ed., *Living with our Hyperactive Children,* with an introduction by John F. Zimmer (New York: Two Continents Publishing Group, Inc., 1977), p. 17.
54. *See Muriel James and Louis Savary, *The Power At the Bottom of the Well* (New York: Harper & Row, 1974), especially chapter 2, "Do You Know that God's Spirit Dwells in You?" pp. 17–32.
54. †Ibid., pp. 17–18. James and Savary distinguish between Eric Berne's concept of the "self" in Transactional Analysis as being the ego state the person is freely expressing at a particular moment, and their own concept of the "spiritual self": "The Inner Core is seen as a permanent personal reality that underlies all three ego states (Parent, Adult, Child)."
54. ‡Carl G. Jung, "The Spiritual Problem of Modern Man," in *The Portable Jung,* ed. Joseph Campbell (New York: Viking Press, 1971), pp. 456–79.
54. §Jung, "Relations Between the Ego and the Unconscious," *Portable Jung,* p. 122.
54. ‖Ibid., p. 79.
55. *See Jung, "Eastern and Western Thinking," *Portable Jung,* especially pp. 487–88.

57. *Ernest Coffin, "I'll Be Laughing," *DAY* (Dialysis and You) magazine, Ernest Coffin Memorial Issue, 3 (1976): 7–10. Mr. Coffin did not finish the above quoted manuscript. He was called to New York for a transplant operation and lived but a short time following the surgery.

57. †Quoted from Louise McCurry, "Another Way of Growing," *DAY* magazine, Ernest Coffin Memorial Issue, 3 (1976): 5–6 (italics by L.G.C.).

58. *Bernard E. Meland, *Higher Education and the Human Spirit* (Chicago: University of Chicago Press, 1953), p. 48.

58. †Eric Berne, *Games People Play* (New York: Grove Press, 1964), p. 15.

59. *Ibid.

59. †Bernard E. Meland, "Narrow is the Way Beyond Absurdity and Anxiety," *Criterion* magazine 15 (Winter 1966): 9.

61. *Seward Hiltner, *Preface to Pastoral Theology* (New York: Abingdon Press, 1958), p. 116.

61. †Ibid., p. 118.

61. ‡*Webster's New International Dictionary,* 3d ed., s.v. "sustain." See the derivation of the word and its definition as determined by the various usages.

62. *See Frederick Perls, Ralph Hefferline, and Paul Goodman, *Gestalt Therapy: Excitement and Growth in the Human Personality* (New York: Julian Press, 1951).

62. †See Muriel James and Dorothy Jongeward, *Born to Win* (New York: Addison Wesley, 1971), especially pp. 242–44.

62. ‡See Carl R. Rogers, *Encounter Groups* (New York: Harper & Row, 1970).

64. *Franz Alexander, *Psychoanalysis and Psychotherapy* (New York: W. W. Norton & Co., 1956), pp. 55–56.

65. *Howard Clinebell, *Basic Types of Pastoral Counseling* (Nashville: Abingdon Press, 1966), pp. 141–44.

65. †Ibid., pp. 143–44.

66. *A description of "The Healing Community," published in pamphlet form in 1976, may be obtained by writing to Harold H. Wilke, 139 Walworth Avenue, White Plains, New York 10606. The original plan called for an effort extended over a period of three years and several months.

66. †Ibid., p. 4.

67. *Ibid., p. 3.

68. *Wilke, " 'Mainstreaming' the Alienated," p. 275.

68. †Ibid.

69. *Ibid.

Social Welfare Services

The handicapped often experience subtle discrimination in regard to disability insurance. They may think they are insured for disability with their company when actually they are not. If an insurance company disallows the disability, the disabled person can appeal to the State Department of Insurance in the state of his or her residence.

Appeals and complaints regarding job-related disabilities can be lodged with the Workmen's Compensation office of the state's industrial board.

Subsidized housing for the handicapped may be obtained by calling the local Housing Counseling office.

Food stamps may be available to handicapped persons. This is a legitimate claim and can be realized by calling appropriate offices. There need be no stigma attached to obtaining food stamps. The program is meant to be helpful to the disabled as well as to poverty-stricken persons.

Easter Seal offices may be contacted for information about services to crippled children.

Most major cities have an information and referral agency that can answer questions about available services. Ask the local telephone operator or call the United Way.

Disability appeals of various kinds can be made through persons designated to handle such appeals. Once again, the pastor may gain such information by calling United Way.

National Organizations

This select list of national organizations serving handicapped persons was compiled from the *Directory of Organizations Interested in the Handicapped,* published by the Committee for the Handicapped/People to People Program, Suite 610, LaSalle Building, Connecticut Avenue and L Street, Washington, DC 20036.

Academy of Dentistry for the
Handicapped
1240 East Main Street
Springfield, OH 45503
(513) 323-0941

Alexander Graham Bell
Association for the Deaf
3417 Volta Place, N.W.
Washington, DC 20007
(202) 337-5220

American Association on
Mental Deficiency
5201 Connecticut Ave., N.W.
Washington, DC 20015
(202) 244-8143

American Association for
Rehabilitation Therapy, Inc.
P.O. Box 93
North Little Rock, AR 72116
(501) 725-9100 Ext. 469

American Cancer Society, Inc.
219 East 42nd Street
New York, NY 10017
(212) 867-3700

American Foundation for the
Blind, Inc.
15 West 16th Street
New York, NY 10011
(212) 924-0420

American Occupational
Therapy Association
6000 Executive Boulevard
Rockville, MD 20852
(301) 770-2200

American Orthotic & Prosthetic
Association
1440 N Street, N.W.
Washington, DC 20005
(202) 234-8400

American Physical Therapy
Association
1156 15th Street, N.W.
Washington, DC 20005
(202) 466-2070

The Arthritis Foundation
1212 Avenue of the Americas
New York, NY 10036
(212) 757-7600

Blinded Veterans Association
1735 DeSales Street, N.W.
Washington, DC 20036
(202) 347-4010

Epilepsy Foundation of
   America
1828 L Street, N.W.
Washington, DC 20036
(202) 293-2930

Federation of the
   Handicapped, Inc.
211 West 14th Street
New York, NY 10011
(212) 242-9050

Muscular Dystrophy
   Associations of America, Inc.
810 Seventh Avenue
New York, NY 10019
(212) 586-0808

National Association
   of the Deaf
814 Thayer Avenue
Silver Spring, MD 20910
(301) 587-1788

National Association of the
   Physically Handicapped, Inc.
6473 Grandville Avenue
Detroit, MI 48228
(313) 271-0160

National Federation
   of the Blind
Suite 212
1346 Connecticut Ave., N.W.
Washington, DC 20036
(202) 785-2974

National Kidney Foundation
116 East 27th Street
New York, NY 10016
(212) 889-2210

National Paraplegia Foundation
333 North Michigan Avenue
Chicago, IL 60601
(312) 346-4779

Paralyzed Veterans of America
7315 Wisconsin Avenue
Suite 301-W
Washington, DC 20014
(301) 652-3464

Placement and Referral Center
   for Handicapped Students,
   Division of Special
   Education & Pupil Personnel
   Services, Board of Education
   of the City of New York
131 Livingston Street
Brooklyn, NY 11201
(212) 624-0854

The President's Committee on
   the Employment of the
   Handicapped
Washington, DC 20210
(202) 961-3401

United Cerebral Palsy
   Association, Inc.
66 East 34th Street
New York, NY 10016
(212) 889-6655

United Ostomy
   Association, Inc.
1111 Wilshire Boulevard
Los Angeles, CA 90017
(213) 481-2811

Annotated Bibliography

Berne, Eric. *Games People Play.* New York: Grove Press, 1964. The first popular publication on Transactional Analysis by the prodigious founder of the system.

Bittinger, Marvin L., ed. *Living with Our Hyperactive Children.* New York: Two Continents Publishing Group, Inc., 1977. A series of stories written by parents regarding their experiences in living with their hyperactive children.

Campbell, Joseph, ed. *The Portable Jung.* New York: Viking Press, 1971. A well-organized publication of Jung's system as extrapolated from his many writings.

Feifel, Herman, ed. *New Meanings of Death.* New York: McGraw-Hill Book Co., 1977. Contributions from psychologists, nurses, physicians, social workers, anthropologists, sociologists, medical and other administrators, professors of law and mortuary science, and patients on their views of death.

Goldstein, Kurt. *The Human Organism.* New York: The American Book Co., 1939. An original statement on the unifying and compensating tendencies of the human organism.

Hiltner, Seward. *Preface to Pastoral Theology.* New York: Abingdon Press, 1958. A systematic presentation by my esteemed mentor and renowned colleague, who is regarded as one of the chief spokesmen for modern pastoral theology.

Kübler-Ross, Elisabeth. *On Death and Dying.* New York: Macmillan, 1969. A classic study of death and dying for multidisciplinary use.

Maslow, Abraham H. *Toward a Psychology of Being.* New York: D. Van Nostrand Co., 1962. A thoughtful and thoroughgoing statement on the psychology of personal growth.

Mooney, Thomas O., Theodore M. Cole, and Richard Chilgren. *Sexual Options for Paraplegics and Quadraplegics.* Boston: Little, Brown, and Co., 1975. A frank and practical presentation of sexuality and sexual techniques for handicapped persons.

Satir, Virginia. *Peoplemaking*. Palo Alto, California: Science and Behavior Books, Inc., 1972. A book for families regarding their intragroup communication.

Tillich, Paul. *The Courage to Be*. New Haven: Yale University Press, 1952. A classic from one of the most creative and constructive theologians of modern times.

The following list of books and notes have been graciously referred to me by Harold H. Wilke who includes them in a course on Ministry with the Physically Handicapped, at Union Theological Seminary, New York.

Baker, Louise. *Out on a Limb*. New York: McGraw-Hill Book Co., 1946. A delightful account of her life as a uniped by a lovely woman who kisses you when, on first being introduced to her, you say, "I know the name—you're the author of *Party Line!*"

Bruckner, Leona. *Triumph of Love*. New York: Simon and Schuster, 1954. A mother's probing analysis of her acceptance of her amputee child.

Brown, Christy. *Down All the Days*. New York: Stein and Day, 1970. A lusty autobiographical novel, lyrical and unsentimental.

Carlson, Earl R. *Born That Way*. New York: John Day Company, 1941. A classic, this medically oriented book recounts the author's own response to cerebral palsy.

Chaput, Richard. *All I Can Give*. Canfield, Ohio: Alba House Communications, 1972. Out of an iron lung, into the world.

Miers, Earl Scheck. *The Trouble Bush*. New York: Rand McNally Co., 1966. A classic autobiography by an historian and English teacher who has published fifty other books as well, felicitious in language and solid in concept.

Steensma, Juliana. *The Quality of Mercy*. Richmond: John Knox Press, 1969. The helpful story of John Steensma at work in Korea.

Wallace, Marjorie, and Michael Robson. *On Giant's Shoulders*. London: Times Books, 1976. The fascinating story of Terry Wiles, one of the most severely handicapped of the "thalidomide babies."

Walker, Turnley. *Rise Up and Walk*. New York: E. P. Dutton, 1950. "Polio is always so unexpected."

Wilke, Harold H. *Strengthened with Might*. Philadelphia: Westminster Press, 1952. A fine statement full of repeatable quotations by a remarkable person.